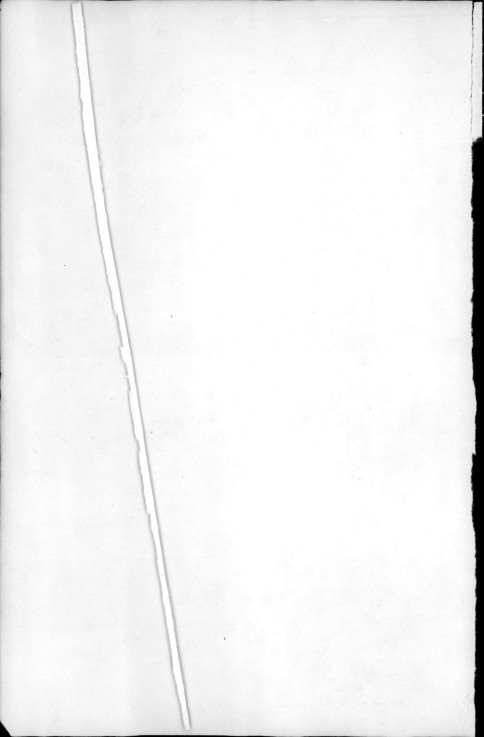

A MURDER IN PARADISE

Books by Richard Gehman

A PARTY AT THE BUCHANAN CLUB
    (*Published as Each Life to Live*)

SARDI'S (*With Vincent Sardi*)

DRIVEN

A MURDER IN PARADISE

A
MURDER
IN
PARADISE

RICHARD GEHMAN

Rinehart and Company, Inc. New York Toronto

*Published Simultaneously in Canada by
Clarke, Irwin & Company, Ltd., Toronto*

*Copyright, 1954, by Richard Gehman
Printed in the United States of America
All Rights Reserved
Library of Congress Catalog Card Number: 54-6376*

TO ESTELLE

Table of Contents

*"I get along with people, I always have,
I always wanted them to like me . . . and
the appalling fact about it now is people
might not like me any more."*

—EDWARD LESTER GIBBS TO DR.
BALDWIN L. KEYES, LANCASTER
COUNTY PRISON, MARCH 10, 1950.

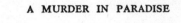

A MURDER IN PARADISE

1

The Crowd and the Victim

The crowd began to form in Grant Street, the alley behind the courthouse, as early as six A.M. on the day of the opening of the trial. The earliest arrivals, mostly men, sat down on the back steps to wait, and when those steps were full, some men went across the alley to sit on the stoops outside the lawyers' offices. A policeman came over from headquarters, which is diagonally across from the back door to the courthouse. He came to keep order, but there was not much for him to do at first. The people, arriving in groups of two and three, were arranging themselves in a line without being ordered, and soon the men came across from the lawyers' stoops and joined the line. Presently the doors to the courthouse were opened, and the line moved up the steps and inside. Two State Policemen halted it at the back stairs to the second floor, the stairs leading up to the large room where the trial was to be heard. Until the doors opened, there had not been a great deal of conversation along the line. Now, indoors, voices began to ring up and down the long, high-ceilinged corridor, and more voices, and more, individual tones blending into a sustained humming and buzzing. Somehow the word was passed around that there would be seats in the courtroom only for about one hundred and fifty spectators, and the noise increased in volume as the crowd pressed forward. By nine o'clock the line stretched east from the rear of the courthouse down the alley all the way to Duke Street, one of the city's main thoroughfares, and far around the corner. A policeman later said there were five hundred people; others declared there were more. Lawyers in their cabinets in the old buildings along Duke Street had trouble concentrating because of the noise, and so did clerks in the county offices.

The crowd came each day the trial was heard. Its character was a matter of constant dispute among those who marveled at its existence. Herb Krone, an old-hand reporter, said later that in some ways the expressions on the faces reminded him of animals. Others said that simple Christian sympathy was plain in the eyes of the waiting line. There were those who contended that it had no character at all, that it was the same crowd which always clustered around the man who fainted on North Queen Street, or turned up in the dawn at the railroad yard to watch the big circus unload. It was composed of a variety of people: some obviously well-to-do, some poorer, some laborers and some businessmen, and even a sprinkling representation of the Mennonites who live in the surrounding county. It was such a typical cross-section that when two Army sergeants turned up one day, one of the local newspapermen was moved to note their presence and ask what they were doing there. "You might say we are just interested in murder trials," one said gruffly. Other people had more explicit reasons: a woman said she felt it was her privilege as an American citizen to

4

attend a public trial and see that justice was done; another man said he was there because he had followed this thing from the very beginning. Everyone who was asked why he had shown up seemed surprised, and perhaps even annoyed, not so much because the question constituted an invasion of privacy, but because the answer should have been so self-evident as to preclude any examination of motive. The mechanics of waiting appeared to interest observers of this crowd more than its existence. It was noted in the papers that some people had gone to considerable trouble to secure positions near the head of the line. A café owner reported that he had spent the night in his automobile in a parking lot a few hundred yards away; although he had had no blankets, he had kept snug by running the heater. He seemed delighted to have thought of this ingenious device. Several of the more provident brought crates and packing cases to sit on. Women took off their shoes to ease their feet. Many carried brown paper bags of sandwiches.

In many ways the trial must have been a disappointment. The majority of the people never even got close to the back door of the courthouse. They did not seem to mind. They came as faithfully as, the following Sunday, they went to church. They came as though some supernatural power with a saturnine sense of humor had maneuvered them there to stand as companionable, giggling, sandwich-munching symbols of certain aspects of our national personality. They came, drawn by a big and exciting vision, and when it failed to materialize they took small substitute pleasures from emotions and rumors that rippled back along their line. They were most rewarded when one of the principal figures in the trial appeared; their tension then could be felt. They vented it once on a woman who swept past the line, past the two silent troopers at the bottom of the stairs; when this happened they voiced an angry, envious protest. They knew how she had managed it. She was rich, and she knew some politicians. It was a sin and a shame that such things could happen. They turned to discussing other things they had heard about her. Some time later, their hunger was somewhat appeased by a man who was directly involved in the trial emotionally. He was an uncle of the victim. He said, in the hearing of several, that he wished he could take the man on trial out by himself and use a club on him. The remark caused a controversy. The noise rose a little, but after a while it died down. The women with their shoes off went back to their conversations and their cardboard cups of soft drink.

In the mornings, when the accused was brought in, and in the afternoons, when he was taken away, the crowd's personal involvement became more noticeable. Police and court officials experienced difficulty getting through to the waiting vehicle. People shouted out words of encouragement and condemnation. Some struggled to see him more closely; others wanted to lay hands on him. Once a woman brushed his sleeve with her finger tips. "Well, I touched him!" she cried, her face bright. "That was enough for me—I touched him!" She looked around triumphantly at those who had not been so fortunate, then bustled off to claim her deserved place as neighborhood heroine. She was not seen again the next day. Another woman, a fat, gray-haired housewife in a faded blue house-coat, with First Reformed compassion in her face, wept whenever they escorted him out. "God love him, God love him," she sobbed, as though in prayer.

On the last day the crowd was almost silent. The sound of shoes on the old stone pavement of the alley seemed louder by contrast. When the accused appeared,

6

those close could easily hear the tearful sniff as he sought to draw mucous back into his nose. There were several minutes of this silence, and then someone could be heard weeping again. The crowd took this as a signal, and dispersed.

In 1951 the death penalty was carried out in Lancaster County, Pennsylvania, as punishment for a crime that had been committed in 1950. It was the trial of the man who committed this crime that drew the crowd described above, and no other crime in Lancaster's history had a more profound, deeper-reaching effect upon its citizens. The principal figures in the case were virtual nonentities; they had no special position in the life of the community, nor were they exceptionally appealing or remarkable or scandalous in any way. Yet it was as though everyone in this rural paradise felt himself personally involved in the case. The crime raised certain fundamental questions in every mind capable of thought: questions of human conduct, of justice, and of the very purpose and position of man upon the earth. Society in Lancaster, represented by the prosecutor and defense attorney, the judge and the jury, resolved these questions, and in so doing raised more. None of the questions has yet been answered or settled to the satisfaction of everyone; possibly none ever will be. Yet their existence tells us something about our state of mind, and perhaps furnishes us with some estimate of what eventually we must learn about ourselves.

The story of this crime begins with a twenty-one-year-old girl named Marian Louise Baker, a sixteen-hundred-dollar-per-year employee in the Treasurer's Office at Franklin and Marshall College. Marian Baker was a tall girl, standing about five feet, nine and one-half inches, and she was well proportioned: she weighed around one hundred and thirty pounds and had mature breasts, broad, rounded hips, and slender legs. Her eyes were brown and her mouth was full. Her complexion was fair; she smiled easily and brightly, and her teeth were in fair repair. She had soft, wavy brown hair, cut short. Except for two visits each year to beauty salons for permanent waves, she was her own hairdresser; on Saturday afternoons, when she went downtown in Lancaster to shop, she wore her hair in pin curlers and attempted to conceal them with a thin silk bandana tied under her incipient double chin. Women in Lancaster often venture downtown with their hair in pin curlers. They walk along the streets hurriedly, their knees knocking together and their eyes cast down, as though if they do not meet the eyes of others, their plastered, iron-studded heads will not be observed. In this way they communicate modesty, propriety and vanity, three highly desirable traits.

Marian Baker was one of these women; she was a naïve girl from the County, with artlessness in her face. The most mildly sophisticated or subtle jokes passed her by, although she pretended that she caught them all. She was highly effective at concealing her naïveté from the boys at Franklin and Marshall—not a great accomplishment, considering, but one which gave her a certain assurance. She employed earthiness in place of wit in a manner that the youths did not grasp, and they thought of her as something of a charmer. Her somewhat soft, rather characterless features were strengthened by a way she had of intimating animal vitality. It was not overt, for outwardly she appeared quite prim and proper in the manner of a girl who had been raised by a County family of faith; it was, rather, a harmless penchant for prankish flirtation. Perhaps it was not even that; it may have been more of a

8

good-natured, rustic spirit which, unwittingly and with no design, implanted in young men certain thoughts which would have embarrassed their subject. For some time Marian was one of the most popular female employees on the campus. Inevitably, she acquired a reputation, constructed for her by boys who wished to assume standing as sports, and to some lesser degree by girls who envied her ability to attract. She was the subject of many a late-at-night debate in fraternity houses and saloons adjacent to the college. No one ever said anything specific about her; no one ever offered evidence. Those who believed the stories about her did not ask proof. They were willing to believe, and unwilling to give up the privilege of whistling as she went by and of experimenting with her in the guilty, furtive privacy of their secret thoughts.

The Marian Louise Baker her close friends knew bore little resemblance to the glamorous, provocative creature who came to life in the pipe smoke of the bull sessions. Born April 10, 1928, she was the daughter of a Mr. and Mrs. Walter Baker, of Perry County, which is located upstate about sixty miles from Lancaster County. When Marian was about six her parents were divorced, and she was taken to live with an aunt, Mrs. Leroy O'Donel, of Conestoga, a hamlet about eight miles south of Lancaster city. The Bakers were country folk, and so were the O'Donels. Leroy, Marian's foster father, was employed at the Safe Harbor dam hydroelectric power plant, from which he took home wages adequate for the comfort of his family. The O'Donels, who had two smaller daughters, regarded Marian as and treated her as one of their own. Her girlhood was emotionally secure, and she grew into a sweet-tempered, lively little thing, known to some of her friends in grade school as a tree-climbing tomboy. Her best chum was a girl named Thelma Kreiter, who lived near by. Thelma called Marian "Wezer," a Lancaster County diminutive for "Louise." The two girls started together in first grade and remained in the same class until both graduated from Manor Township High, a consolidated school located in Millersville.

Thelma, today Mrs. John Weaver, remembers Marian as a good student, popular with boys and girls alike, one who could make friends with practically anybody. Because she had to take the school bus back to Conestoga every day, Marian could not participate in as many extracurricular activities as she would have liked, but she was elected president of a class club and was an enthusiastic supporter of the school's varsity track and basketball teams. Marian graduated from Manor June 3, 1946. *The Trumpeter,* the school yearbook, said of her,

". . . that sweet miss from Conestoga. An all-around pal. . . . She takes great interest in her studies but they never keep her from being elsewhere at times. We wonder why 'Wezer' is always so eager to visit her grandmother????"

Marian had taken the commercial course at Manor. The week after graduation she applied for work at Hamilton Watch Company, and shortly thereafter was hired as a cashier in the cafeteria. She worked there three months, commuting on the bus from Conestoga. At this time, she was not "going steady" (as she would have put it) with any particular boy, but she was as popular with her fellow workers at Hamilton as she had been in school. She was a generous, warm-hearted girl; everyone said so. "She seemed to get a real kick out of doing little favors for people," a man who worked with her has recalled.

Marian might have stayed on at the watch factory indefinitely if it had not been for a telephone call from the office of the principal at Manor High. The call informed her that a man named Donald M. Mylin, Treasurer at Franklin and Marshall College, was looking for a girl to be a secretary in his office. Mylin was a part-time neighbor of the O'Donels; he had a summer place a few miles up the road. On the evening of the day she received the call, Marian walked over to the Mylin property. She found her future employer, a short, slight, white-haired man of medium height, perched on a pole in the barnyard. He was fixing some electrical wires. When she called up to introduce herself, he shinnied down the pole and took her into the house to meet his wife. Together the Mylins questioned her, and they were impressed by her ready answers, her quiet respect, and her neatness. At the end of the interview, Mylin told her the job was hers if she wanted it.

Two weeks later, after working out her notice at Hamilton, Marian reported for work at Franklin and Marshall. She loved it there from the very beginning. For one thing, the work was simple. She did a little typing, and she acted as cashier; she stood at a small counter at the front of the office and cashed checks for or collected money for bills from the students. The job was not like a job at all, she often said; it was more play than anything else. The young men who came in liked to joke with her, and she joked right back. She had a memory for names which astonished Mylin and Mrs. Nancy Stonesifer, an assistant professor's wife who also worked in the office. She had only to meet a student once; next time she remembered his name. Some of the boys took to making frequent trips to Mylin's office on one pretext or another, and once they had completed their transactions they would linger around the counter, prolonging the conversation. One of these boys was a married student whom everyone called Eddie Gibbs. He did not joke as much as the others did, but he was no less talkative: he kept Marian up to date on his car, he told her how much he had paid for a new suit, he discussed his marks and he passed opinions on various teachers. Marian seldom, if ever, discussed the boys with Mrs. Stonesifer, but one day, after Gibbs had been hanging around for a half hour, she confided that Gibbs' continual chatter about himself made her sick.

Some of the girls who worked at F. & M. could not explain exactly what it was about Marian that made the boys flock to her. She dressed quietly, most often in plaid skirts and white blouses, and only occasionally in a sweater which outlined her breasts. Her taste in clothes was that of the average County high-school girl, and she sometimes wore frilly, feminine things which were not quite right for a girl as tall as she. Her modest education and County upbringing were apparent in her speech. She used such Pennsylvania Dutch localisms as "The money is all," meaning it was all gone, and she spoke of brown-skinned people as "dark-complected." She was regarded—and regarded herself—as a fast girl on the uptake. One day Assistant Professor Richard Stonesifer came into the office to confer with his wife. As he was leaving, he stumbled over the threshold. Marian, without looking up from her typewriter, said, "Dick, I'll have a red sign painted there the next time you come in." One of her friends has offered this as an example of her quick wit.

Marian began going out with students shortly after she began working at the college. She never went long with any one. Donald Mylin remembers that the boys she dated were, for the most part, "nice, clean-cut boys, not wolves or anything like that." Mylin had a fatherly interest in his new employee, and he was openly fond of her. This caused some small resentment among the other girls in the office, for there were times when Marian neglected her work either to read *True Confessions,* her favorite magazine, or to visit another college office where a close friend, Dottie Shaub, was employed. Sometimes she brought some of Dottie's typing back to the treasurer's office and worked on it while her own work went untouched. She and Mrs. Stonesifer had several arguments about this, and there was one period in which they did not speak to each other for several months. Mylin ignored the argument. He treated both girls with affection and kindness, but he did lean somewhat in Marian's favor, most probably because she was a neighbor and often rode to work with him in his car. On Sunday afternoons, when she had a date with a new young man, she would stroll by Mylin's house to show him off. She looked upon Mylin and his wife as a second set of parents.

Marian worked in the treasurer's office nearly four years. By her second year her name as a lively, available number was firmly established on the campus. There is some question as to whether this reputation was deserved. In an investigation of Marian's habits and character, police officers were unable to establish her promiscuity. Those who knew her well are convinced that she was the victim of those rumors and innuendoes upon which many Lancastrians seem to thrive. Discussing her, her best friend, Mrs. John Weaver, has said, "Marian liked good, clean fun. I never thought she did anything out of the road, not like they said. She never had any care for advances of any type made on her. If somebody ever did something or suggested something she would tell you in a very few words what she thought of it. She went to some college parties, but although she told me everything when she came home she never gave any indication that she was promiscuous." One girl who attended a fraternity house party at which Marian was present recalls that she arrived with her face flushed, and that she said, in a loud voice, that she'd had too much to drink (she seldom, almost never, drank). After one drink at the party, she retired to a darkened room, lay down on a couch, and fell asleep. She slept all through the party and awoke in some embarrassment. Then, when she saw that everyone regarded it as a joke, she laughed along with the rest.

During the latter part of 1949, Marian began going out with a young Conestoga neighbor of hers. His name was Edgar Rankin. He was a personable, friendly, dark-haired young man who worked at Armstrong Cork in Lancaster. The two got on well from the beginning, and Donald Mylin observed to his wife, when Marian brought Edgar around to the house, that it looked as though this might be a little more serious than the previous romances. After a short time Marian stopped going out with all other boys. There was only one point of disagreement between the couple. Rankin liked the companionship of men, and he sometimes would show up late for a date because he had stopped off for a drink or two with the boys. But, after a while, he became more punctual. At Christmas time, he gave her an engagement ring. It was a small solitaire purchased from Kay's, a credit jeweler, but in Marian's view it might have come from Tiffany's. Donald Mylin recalls the first day she wore her ring to work:

"When she came in, she wanted me to see it, I could tell that, and I did see it, but I teased her. I pretended I didn't. She kept trying to attract my attention to it, putting her hand on the desk, looking at her hand, and so on, and finally I said to her, 'It looks as though you were down to the ten-cent store.' She blushed, and she was all smiles."

Rankin and Marian set no date for their wedding, but they began making vague plans. He turned up at her

14

house every night. By that time he had been placed on a night shift, and his arrivals and departures sometimes awakened the O'Donel household. So as not to inconvenience her foster parents, Marian accepted Mrs. John Weaver's invitation to move into the city and live with her and her husband. The Weavers had a house at 415 Reynolds Avenue, one of a block-long row of identical brick structures with wooden front porches. Marian was given a room of her own, and she loved living there. She felt that at last her life was her own, and she told Mrs. Weaver that she sometimes dreamed of the day when she and Ed would have a place of their own. In the evenings, when she had no date, she sometimes practiced cooking in the kitchen, and she and Mrs. Weaver had many long talks about homely problems. Once she bought a scrapbook in which she planned to paste pictures of herself and Rankin, but she never got around to mounting the snapshots.

On the morning of Tuesday, January 10, 1950, Marian Louise Baker awakened in excellent spirits. She was looking forward to two things that day: she was to pick up her ring at Kay's, where she had taken it to have the stone more securely fastened in the bezel, and she had an appointment for a permanent wave at five thirty P.M. Mrs. Weaver noticed that she sang and hummed as she was getting ready for work. She put on a white blouse, a blue, black and white plaid skirt, stockings, and low black suede shoes with overhanging tongues and crepe soles. Over this she wore her red, green and black plaid coat. She loved plaids.

At the office, Mrs. Nancy Stonesifer also noticed that Marian seemed exceptionally cheerful. By this time the two girls had resolved their differences and were quite companionable. While Marian was cashing checks and going about her business at the front counter, Mrs. Stonesifer made out a bank-deposit slip which Marian was to take downtown later in the day. Carrying checks to the bank was part of her daily routine. Around ten that morning, activity in the office quieted. Mrs. Stonesifer, who had her hair in curlers, asked Marian if she would help her take it down. The two girls retired to the ladies' room and lighted cigarettes (only professors are permitted to smoke in their offices at Franklin and Marshall). They chatted aimlessly about inconsequential matters while Marian combed out Mrs. Stonesifer's hair.

Mrs. Stonesifer went to lunch around eleven thirty A.M. When she returned, Marian had gone to lunch. Marian came back around one thirty P.M. She sat down at her desk without removing her coat, complaining that she was so rushed with work all of a sudden that she wished she did not have to go to the bank. She was afraid she might be late for her appointment at the beauty parlor. Mrs. Stonesifer gave her a letter she had written to a Canadian bank and asked her to mail it at the post office. Marian picked up her pocketbook, a leather pouch purse, and remarked that she had left her umbrella at the college cafeteria. She and Mrs. Stonesifer laughed together; Marian's habit of losing umbrellas had become a standing joke between them.

Marian took a College Avenue bus from the corner of West James Street and College Avenue, and rode downtown to Penn Square, the center of the city. First she picked up her ring at Kay's, which is located a few steps off the Square, and then walked one block east to the Farmers' Bank, which stands on the corner of East King and South Duke Streets, directly opposite the Lancaster County courthouse. She arrived at the bank at approximately one fifty P.M. and went to the window of a teller's cage occupied by Mrs. Hope Renninger, an acquaintance. There she made her deposit, which totaled approximately seventy dollars and was entirely in checks. She and Mrs. Renninger chatted briefly, and she displayed her engagement ring. She said, "Tomorrow when I come in you won't recognize me—I'm having my hair done this afternoon." "Isn't that nice," said Mrs. Renninger.

Marian left the bank, walked west to Penn Square, and turned up North Queen Street, which she followed two blocks north to the corner where Chestnut intersects it. There she turned west and walked a half block to the post office. She registered and mailed the letter Mrs. Stonesifer had given her, and proceeded on through the lobby toward the western exit. At approximately two six P.M., Percy Leroy Campbell, a clerk at the STAMPS WHOLESALE window, came back from lunch, raised his blind, and saw her going by. Campbell knew her well. He was a resident of Conestoga, for one thing, and for another she often bought stamps for the office from him. He waved to her, and she raised her left arm to him in what he later described as a "high ball."

Marian continued out of the post office. Going down the steps, she met George Crudden, a newspaperman, who also holds a part-time job as sports publicist for Franklin and Marshall. Crudden greeted her, and she answered him. The meeting made so little impression upon Crudden that he cannot, today, remember exactly what they said to each other. He does not even recall which end of the post office it was.

Except for one other person, George Crudden was the last ever to speak to Marian Louise Baker.

2

The Scene

Lancaster County, Pennsylvania, is a roughly triangular area covering 941 square miles in the southeastern part of the state. The locale in many respects resembles many others throughout the land; it could be called "typical," if that word were not too dangerously inclusive. The people who live there are not too dissimilar, broadly speaking, from the people in every other state.

This area is popularly referred to as "America's Garden Spot." The nickname is deserved; ever since the settlers came there in the early 1700's, the land has given up a rich annual harvest. The population of the County is around two hundred and thirty-five thousand. Its bank resources in 1951 amounted to $243,379,096. Not all of the wealth comes from the soil; in the County seat, the city of Lancaster, there are large manufacturing plants—Armstrong Cork and Hamilton Watch have their headquarters there, and there are branches of Radio Corporation of America and Aluminum Corporation of America. Despite these relatively new industrial developments, the

County has remained primarily agricultural in character. For years it was known as the second richest farm section in the United States, and it has always led all other counties in the nation in production of tobacco. The Lancaster city municipal markets, where the Countians bring their produce three days each week, have been famous for decades; they set the pattern for similar markets in other communities. The County is as beautiful as it is rich. Its fertile soil is distributed over gently sloping hills, crossed by swift, clear little brooks and leisurely creeks. Some of the hills are wooded; some are matted with briars and bushes in which small animals and birds make their homes. There are thousands of acres of green pastureland to which steers from Western ranches are sent to be finished before going to market. The majority of the gray stone and white frame farmhouses are very old, and so are their attendant barns, silos and outbuildings. Many of these rural estates have been in the same families for generations, and aspiring farmers from the city have always had a difficult time prying land from the natives. There is a wonderfully serene quality about this countryside, and a picture shot at random almost anywhere could stand as an idealized, stylized representation of agrarian scenery. Appropriately enough, some early landowners named one Lancaster County hamlet "Paradise."

To the rest of the country, Lancaster County is known principally as one of the centers of the Amish and Mennonites, those severely dressed, severely religious sects who have been known immemorially as "plain people." Offshoots of the Anabaptists, they came into being in central and western Europe during the sixteenth century. They pride themselves today upon their anachronistic customs and costumes. In reality, they have little to do with the mainstream of life in Lancaster County, although

19

the area is associated with them in the minds of out-landers because local promoters have capitalized upon their quaintness and made them into a tourist attraction. In recent years the Pennsylvania Dutch (a misnomer, because not all Pennsylvania Dutch are "plain" people) have become big business. Shops in Lancaster city and County are crammed with "Amish" and "Mennonite" souvenirs—gaily decorated ash trays, trivets, book ends, dolls, dishes and furniture—most of them as alien to the sects as the use of electricity, which the Amish forbid themselves. There are only about three thousand Amish in Lancaster County, concentrated around a series of villages bearing such names as Blue Ball, Bareville, Bird-in-Hand and Intercourse (the latter is close to Paradise, and there is an old joke about their juxtaposition). Illinois and Ohio have larger "plain" colonies than Lancaster County's. In addition to these sects, which came from Switzerland and the Palatinate, the County was settled by Germans, Scotch-Irish, some Welsh and a sprinkling of English, predominately Protestant. Religion is still a primary force in the lives of the people, as evinced by the seventy-eight churches in Lancaster city, which in the 1950 census had a population of 63,774. The citizens are strict conformists, by and large, which leads some into grace, some into hypocrisy, and others, as may be concluded presently, into a well-meaning misinterpretation of Christian principle. Neither religious intolerance nor racial and religious prejudice are unknown to these God-fearing people, nor is class consciousness. In Lancaster city there are three country clubs, none of which can claim more than a tiny percentage of Catholics and Jews in its membership list, and at least one of which was formed, according to local intelligence, because too many Jews were turning up at the pay-as-you-play public links where the club members formerly foregathered. The Negro population of the County totals less than 1800. Negroes are treated better, on the whole, than other minorities, possibly because they stay strictly to themselves in Lancaster city's slum section, the Seventh Ward, known as The Bloody Seventh. Norwood (Barney) Ewell, the reknowned sprinter, came out of that neighborhood to win several A.A.U. and Olympic championships some years ago. He was honored upon his triumphal return to Lancaster with a "Barney Ewell Day," in which he was given the adulation of the community and a furnished house. Ewell's was a begrudged eminence, in essence; his race is still inferior in the Lancaster mind. The breakdown of social and racial barriers which is slowly occurring in this slowly maturing country may well hit Lancaster County with full force about the time it hits Boston.

As the farmers set out their crops in strips and plots, so the people of Lancaster County arrange their lives. They are methodical, meticulous people, dedicatedly set in their ways, creatures of rigid routine which is rooted in religion, in money, and in the folkways of their fathers and grandfathers. Some even cling to the Pennsylvania Dutch dialect, a humorously utilitarian hybrid of German and English, speaking it in their homes and in the markets, but even those who speak the American language exclusively, and who have become thoroughly third-generation-Americanized, are slow to react to new ideas and slower to change their minds and manners. Superstition still exists; the hex signs on barns are for decoration, of course, but as an old Pennsylvania Dutchman once remarked to a friend, some of the signs may be there because it doesn't pay to take chances. Homely ideas about physiology still prevail: there are many who will not eat ice cream after eating fish. Chiropractors, faith healers and powwow doctors administer to segments of the population. Wild-eyed, crack-voiced evangelists take off high scores in tents during the summers. In politics, the most conservative wing of the Republican party holds sway, personified by a cigar-smoking committeeman with a vaudeville Dutch accent; in business, no virtue is more highly regarded than caution. The people live prosperously and punctiliously. They eat their dinners in the middle of the day, and they eat heartily. Every young man and woman puts on five pounds soon after getting married, and continues to gain as the well-fed years go by. Houses in Lancaster run to spacious detached units, two and three stories tall, of brick or frame, or to rows of similar boxes running the length of a block. The larger detached dwellings have been converted to apartments in great numbers since the beginning of World War II. Even the majority of row houses have front porches. There are so many trees—oaks, elms, maples, sycamores, among others —that from the top of the Griest Building, the city's tallest building (fifteen stories), the city appears to have been built in a forest. There will be even more trees within the next few years, for a tree-planting committee has recently been formed. Lancaster is a city of leaf-burners, sidewalk-sweepers, and stoop-scrubbers. Women who emerge in the early mornings to polish the brass knobs on wrought-iron porch railings sometimes wear large sunbonnets; they resemble the old lady on the Old Dutch Cleanser can. They carry this passion for tidiness into their personal lives, too. They get to appointments exactly on time, transporting themselves in new cars for which they traded in the year-before-last's model. The cars often carry above the rear license plate a tiny metal plate saying *Jesus Saves,* and in the County the road-warning signs are punctuated by crudely lettered signs that warn motorists: PREPARE

TO MEET THY GOD. For diversion the people have church, the movies, the taprooms (many of which still have signs saying "Tables for Ladies"), miniature golf courses, fire company carnivals, school festivals, stock-car racing, "chicken corn soup suppers," turkey shoots, bowling, public sales, ox roasts, fishing on the Susquehanna (ten to fifteen miles from the city), professional wrestling, Sunday night floor shows at American Legion homes, shuffleboard in bars, horseshoes in backyards, dances in parks and Moose auditoriums, testimonial dinners for embarrassed elder citizens, family reunions, spectator and participating sports, hillbilly square dances, hymn sings, hot-rodding over the back roads, television and gossip. Until recently there was a pitifully inadequate public library, but funds have finally been collected after years of effort, and a new one is being built. The library at Franklin and Marshall College is an excellent one, and so is that of Millersville State Teachers College, four miles outside the city, but a remark heard frequently is "I never get much time to read." Mickey Spillane's books sell well at the downtown newsstands; so do those of Cornell Woolrich, Frank Yerby, and other members of the violence-and-lust schools. There is one store that sells books exclusively in the city, Barr-Hurst, now operated by a retired umbrella manufacturer named John Hartman. At Millersville, the administration has encouraged an English professor named Lynwood Lingenfelter to bring in writers, poets, and historians for a series of lectures.

F. & M. and M.S.T.C. are two of four institutions of higher education in the County; the other two are Elizabethtown College, located in a village about eighteen miles west of the city; and the Theological Seminary of the Evangelical and Reformed Church in the United States, which is across College Avenue from the campus of Franklin and Marshall. The latter, a small liberal arts college for men (the current enrollment hovers around one thousand), was formed in 1853 by the merger of two older schools—Franklin College, founded in 1787, and named for Benjamin Franklin, who was actively interested in it, and Marshall College, founded in 1836 at Mercersburg, Pennsylvania, and named for John Marshall. James Buchanan, the fifteenth President of the United States, was first president of the Board of Trustees of the new college; Buchanan's home, "Wheatland," is located a few blocks southeast of the campus. It has been restored and is a popular tourist attraction. The college has always played an important part in the cultural life of the city, but it would not be accurate to call Lancaster a college town. The percentage of day students is not very high. Thanks to the college's Green Room Club, an amateur dramatic organization directed by a brilliant and irascible transplanted Westerner named Darrell Larsen, the theater has flourished in Lancaster during the past quarter century. It has always been a good theater town, in fact; John Durang, the first native American actor, was born in Lancaster, and from the late 1890's to the early 1920's the old Fulton Opera House, now a second-run movie theater, was host to better traveling companies. There has been a movement initiated to make the Fulton a kind of national museum of the theater. Today the County is visited chiefly by musical variety organizations, such as those of Fred Waring or Horace Heidt, and then only for one-night stands; but there is legitimate theater in Philadelphia, sixty-odd miles to the east, and in Baltimore, seventy-odd miles southeast, both of which get Broadway shows in pre- or post-New York engagements. Several artists of distinction live in the County; the late Charles Demuth came from a local family, one branch of which still runs

24

the oldest tobacco shop in the United States, founded by an ancestor before the Revolution. The shop, Demuth's, still stands in East King Street, diagonally southeast of the courthouse, in its original building. The city also claims the oldest department store (Hager's), and the oldest hardware store (Steinman's). There are three or four writers living in the county, and a composer or two. There is a Lancaster Symphony, employing an out-of-town conductor, and a Community Concert Association.

The county played an important part in the making of the nation, and there is a small museum and an active Historical Society with an excellent collection of ancient documents. The city, one of the oldest inland settlements, was founded as Hickory Town in 1718, and given the name Lancaster in 1729 by John Wright, who had come from Lancashire in England. William Penn's representatives signed an agreement with the Indians in the old Moravian Church on Orange Street, and the Continental Congress sat in Lancaster when Philadelphia was captured by the British. The Cloisters at Ephrata, in the County, were used as hospitals for the wounded during the Revolution. The Kentucky long rifle and the Conestoga wagon, among the most useful instruments in the opening up of the West, both were manufactured in Lancaster County. Robert Fulton's birthplace is located there. The entire area is full of landmarks with historical meaning. The Chamber of Commerce makes much of these ties with the past; the people, for the most part, simply live with them, more often than not forgetting that they are there except on national holidays or local anniversaries. In one sense, this is part of the cachet of the Lancastrian. He lives, he goes about his business, concerned with getting through each day. He is content with his family, his business, and his church, he rather resents outsiders, and he is not overly concerned with the happenings of the world except insofar as they directly threaten his earning power or comfort. These are broad statements; they do not apply to everyone. But if a perfectly representative Lancastrian could be miraculously compounded in terms of these aspects of character, it would be discovered that large parts of him exist in all his brothers, ranging from the County tenant farmers up to the people who live in the old, baronial estates on the western edge of the city, and from the most stupid, primitive Amishman up to the leader of the County's intellectuals.

As might be expected, there is not much crime in Lancaster. Policemen in New York, who make around one hundred and forty thousand arrests and write out roughly one million summonses annually, have a departmental expression that goes, "If we don't get you one year, we'll get you the next"; a Lancaster cop or county constable would have as much difficulty grasping this figure as a grocer in Peach Bottom, one of the county hamlets, would have trying to imagine the yearly business of the A. & P. The Lancaster city force makes around 1900 arrests each year. Under Commissioner Fred G. McCartney, a retired member of the Pennsylvania State Police, the seventy-four-man force is a highly efficient one. The police are human beings; they are kindly, courteous and businesslike, with the inevitable one or two ill-tempered exceptions. The low incidence of crime is undoubtedly due in part to their commendable execution of their day-to-day duties. Organized crime has never managed to get a foothold in Lancaster. During Prohibition days a few bootleggers operated in the city, banded together for mutual protection, but if there is any kind of mob in existence today, it must be made up of lazy, peaceable men who move like wraiths. The payola is as foreign to this community as, say, polygamy. There is one cardroom in the city, but it is chartered as a social club. From time to time, fugitives from big-city gangs, on the lam out of fear or ennui, turn up and take rooms in the cheaper hotels, to spend their days lounging along the sidewalks, chewing gum and reading the racing sheets, but the absence of night life, and the difficulty of getting down a bet (the handbooks are closed) soon sends them on to livelier hideouts. Occasionally one will see in a North Queen Street trap a girl who might be taken for a prostitute, but she more likely will be a native of one of the County towns, painted loudly and dressed in pitiful scraps of old rhinestoned *crepe de chine,* daring to look for the forbidden romance she has read about in magazines in the beauty shop that lacquered her croquinole wave. Men who are arrested on narcotics raps are invariably out-of-towners. At intervals, itinerant thieves come to town to ply their trade; to some long-suffering, trusting merchants, whose innate faith in people has caused them to be taken again and again, the intervals must seem regular. Last spring a band of forgers moved in, deposited a small sum in a bank, rented an office, and set up a phony floor-covering company. After a little while they methodically laid their paper, using salary checks made out to themselves. Then they quietly moved on, taking with them more than a thousand dollars. Local crimes and misdemeanors run to the common variety of deeds done everywhere in the country by greedy, desperate, driven, or merely mischievous people; there is almost never a crime notable for its brutality or imaginativeness. During the past twenty years there have been two cases of embezzlement of funds, each the act of a trusted bank employee, the one a trapped horseplayer. Within the past three years a combine of junkmen systematically fleeced a local plant in selling and reselling salvage, but the ring was discovered and broken up. There are never many murders, and when one occurs it usually is committed by some feeble-minded member of the poorer classes, who invariably throws himself on the mercy of the court and gets a lenient sentence, usually ten to twenty years. According to Chief of Detectives John Kirchner, for thirty-two years a member of the Lancaster force, there was only one murder in 1952. Murders in Lancaster have never been marked by extreme cruelty, or elaborate planning; more often than not they have been open-and-shut cases, quickly dispatched by the courts. Capital punishment is rare. The first instance occurred in 1770, when a man named Jockey Jones was hanged in the County for horse thievery. Hanging was the means of the death penalty in Pennsylvania until 1915, when the electric chair came into use. Between 1915 and 1922, only seven men were electrocuted after they had been sentenced to death by the County courts. After 1922, Lancaster juries showed a striking lenience in dealing with murderers, a merciful attitude which may have been connected with the religious nature of the county. Between 1922 and 1951, not a single person was sentenced to death. Until 1950, no jury in Lancaster ever came forth from its chambers with an actual recommendation of the death penalty.

3

The Search and the Discovery

At eight thirty A.M. on Wednesday, January eleventh, the treasurer's office seemed strangely quiet. The cream-colored walls, the oak-stained paneling, the three safes, the gas-station calendars, the coat tree, the four desks facing each other in pairs, and the long battery of filing cabinets were still and somehow ominous, like a *trompe l'oeil* of anticipated tragedy. Nancy Stonesifer was first to work that morning. Her eyes fell immediately upon the desk and chair where Marian Baker customarily worked. She thought quickly of the previous afternoon when Marian had failed to come back from the bank and had not called in. She could not help feeling a twinge of worry. Donald Mylin arrived soon afterward. He and Mrs. Stonesifer looked at the empty desk and at each other. Mylin is a short, sturdy man with gray-white hair and a placid face. He is not easily excited. He said quietly, "Maybe you ought to call Mrs. Weaver," and began going through some papers on his desk.

Mrs. Stonesifer dialed the number of Armstrong

Cork and located the section in which Mrs. John Weaver was then employed. Mrs. Weaver was called to the telephone. She did not sound concerned. "Well," she said, "she *did* have that appointment at the beauty parlor. I thought she was going down there with Dottie Shaub. Maybe they met Ed and he took them out to Dottie's house. I tell you what, I'll call Mrs. O'Donel. Maybe she went out there last night."

Putting down the telephone, Mrs. Stonesifer thought, Surely we're all worried over nothing; surely she'll come walking in any minute now. But when she addressed Mylin, her words seemed to lend substance to her fears.

"She wasn't at the Weavers' last night."

Mylin looked at his hands. "Try her aunt and uncle."

"I thought I might call Dottie Shaub," Mrs. Stonesifer said.

Dottie Shaub had not seen Marian the day before, and had not heard from her. Mrs. Weaver called back, now plainly worried. The O'Donels had neither seen Marian nor heard from her. The family of Edgar Rankin had neither seen nor heard from her. Rankin himself had neither seen nor heard from her. He had been with her Sunday night, and had promised to call her sometime during the week.

Leroy O'Donel called Donald Mylin and, in a voice that broke slightly, summed up the dismal evidence of countless calls and checks and inquiries. "Mr. Mylin," he said, "Marian doesn't seem to be anywhere."

Mylin immediately called city police headquarters and was put through to Captain John Kirchner. He repeated O'Donel's remark, and calmly answered Kirchner's careful, detailed questions. He described Marian and told what he believed she had done after leaving the college the day before. He said he thought she had gone to the bank, the jewelry store and the post office. He said he thought she might have gone directly to the beauty salon instead of returning to the college. When he put down the telephone, he and Mrs. Stonesifer again tried to reassure each other, telling themselves they were getting upset over nothing. Yet there sat the empty desk and the empty chair, refuting their reassurances.

Captain John Kirchner is a heavy-set, stolid man, with a red face and eyes that tell nothing of his thoughts. In his years on the force he has handled cases of every kind, and he has developed the veteran policeman's intuition for disaster. He later told an acquaintance that he felt uneasy as he heard Mylin talking. When the conversation was over he stared for some minutes at the information he had written down. His heavy hands straightened the paper so that its edge was exactly parallel to the edge of his desk. Then he set his machinery to work. A thirteen-state police teletype alarm went out in a matter of minutes. The State Police were enlisted. Captain Kirchner pulled all his men off the jobs they were working on and dispatched them to question everyone they could find who had known Marian Louise Baker and who might have seen her on the preceding day.

The detectives began coming back to report late in the afternoon. "The uncle is very worried," one said. "He's afraid something's happened to her. He says she's never been gone for any length of time without notifying them. He says she never had many boyfriends, and she didn't reach the serious stage with boys until she began dating this Rankin." The detective who had been questioning people at Franklin and Marshall had a slightly different version. He reported the many dates she had had with boys on the campus. Two young men had once stolen the college car to go out to Conestoga to see her late at night;

they had been temporarily suspended from school for the prank. This detective later described her to reporters as "definitely a party girl." But, the detective added, there was nothing to indicate that the girl had been promiscuous. Listening to the reports, Captain Kirchner ruled out the possibility of suicide. The girl had been in good health and evidently had not a worry in the world. Since Christmas, when her engagement had been announced, she had been in exceptionally good spirits. Captain Kirchner's uneasiness began to increase.

On Wednesday night the police sped to check a report which at first appeared to be a lead. Someone called to say that an automobile, seen in the vicinity of Woods Avenue on the western edge of the city, had contained a girl who cried out as though she were being molested. Police made a thorough canvass of the Woods Avenue section, calling at each house. They turned up nothing. The report had been too vague in the first place.

On Thursday the searchers intensified their efforts. Detective Al Farkas and Policewoman Alice Rubicam had determined by systematic questioning of various people that the girl had last been seen around two fifteen P.M. by George Crudden. Farkas was somewhat handicapped in his work at this time; he had broken a leg, and had to get about on crutches. Now the Commissioner ordered an exhaustive search of all empty lots, alleys, petting spots, streams and empty buildings in the city. Meanwhile the State Police were looking into all back roads, lanes and wooded sections in the County. Police near New Bloomfield, Pennsylvania, went to see Mrs. Bruce Britcher, Marian's mother; she told them she had not seen her daughter since the preceding October. They questioned the girl's father, Walter Baker, who told them he had not seen her for "some time." He added that he had seen her only a few times since he and his wife had been separated.

Thursday afternoon, Captain Kirchner sat in his office and faced a reporter blankly. "You can put in that I am very much worried about this case," he said. "It doesn't have the earmarks of someone who voluntarily left town." He and his men had two theories. The missing girl possibly had been a victim of amnesia; or perhaps she had accepted a ride from some stranger, someone she thought she knew.

The Captain did not reveal his principal source of worry. That day, Fred Erb, proprietor of a gasoline service station located about three miles east of Lancaster on Route 30, the Lincoln Highway, had found a black onyx ring in the drain pipe of his men's room. The ring was identified as Marian Baker's. Police could see no reason for the girl to have been in a men's room; they felt certain that if she had lost the ring, she would have reported it to Erb.

Early on Friday the thirteenth, police thought they had another lead. A woman named Mrs. Isabel Anadio, proprietress of a sandwich shop on Baltimore Avenue in Philadelphia, called police there to report that a girl answering to Marian Baker's description had appeared in her shop on Wednesday evening. The girl had ordered a sandwich and a cup of coffee, Mrs. Anadio said, and as she was opening her purse to pay the check, she had dropped a bus token on the floor. She had left without bothering to pick it up. The token was one issued by the Conestoga Traction Company, the Lancaster bus authority. Philadelphia police showed Mrs. Anadio a photograph of Marian Baker.

"Yes," she said, positively, "that's the girl."

Unfortunately, Mrs. Anadio was unable to say where the girl had gone upon leaving the shop. Police thus had no more to work on than they'd had before. The report brought some hope to Leroy O'Donel. He said he believed that Marian had dropped the token as a clue; he was sure she had been kidnaped, and that the kidnaper had allowed her to go in the shop to get some food. Edgar Rankin disagreed; he did not believe the girl had been Marian. Rankin had been questioned and cross-questioned so many times by policemen he was nearly exhausted. A photograph taken at the time shows him staring at a handful of snapshots of his fiancée, bewilderment and apprehension dominating his face. In the photograph he is wearing a baseball cap.

Immediately after the Anadio report came in, police checked a friend of Marian Baker's, Sylvia Newkirk, who lived on Lansdowne Avenue in Philadelphia. Miss Newkirk had not seen her, and had not heard from her for some time. Then police ran into what they thought might develop into another lead. Around the college they learned that before she had begun going about with Rankin, Marian had had several dates with a young man from New Jersey. The boy had since left college. Police learned that he had been married for more than a year and had not been away from home during the preceding two weeks.

Now State Police began stopping all cars along the main highways and some back roads. Two more false leads turned up within a short time. It was reported that in Honey Brook, Pennsylvania, twenty-odd miles from the city, a girl had been heard screaming in an automobile which also contained three men. That had happened around nine thirty P.M. Tuesday, the day of Marian Baker's disappearance. Nobody had obtained the car's license number. In Harrisburg, about thirty-six miles from

Lancaster, a sixty-two-year-old retired janitor named Isaac H. Kuhn told police that on Thursday night, while sitting in the bus terminal, he had seen a young girl answering to Marian Baker's description get off a bus and leave the station, accompanied by a redheaded girl. Kuhn could furnish no further information.

On Friday, at the urging of the officers, Donald Mylin carefully checked the books Marian had kept in the office. He found nothing out of order; as usual, they were neatly and scrupulously balanced. He said, "I have always been so sure of her I didn't even bother to make the check until today." Thus any possibility of Marian's having made off with funds was ruled out.

By Saturday at noon the police had made no further progress. Captain Kirchner was beginning to despair of solving the case. That afternoon, his worst fears were substantiated.

Around the time that most people in Lancaster were sitting down to their Saturday dinners, Mr. and Mrs. Martin Mylin Harnish looked out the window of their home, saw that it was a nice day, and decided to drive out to their summer cottage for a walk in the woods, as they often did on fine afternoons. They were particularly anxious to make the visit because they were planning a trip to Florida and were to leave on the following Monday. They wanted to have one final look around. Harnish is a respected attorney; his wife, Frances, is an intelligent, active woman, prominent in civic affairs. They live modestly in West Walnut Street, in a quiet residential section of the city, and spend weekends and summers in a small frame cottage on a little farm in West Lampeter Township, about five miles south of the city. The cottage is located in a small wood across Mill Creek from the Media Heights Golf Club, one of the three country clubs in Lancaster. This wood is cut through by a number of driveways and lanes, and used to be a favorite parking place for lovers. The Harnish family cottage faces approximately east, and a small driveway loops around in front of it. On the west there is a sloping hill.

Mr. and Mrs. Harnish drove out to their cottage around three thirty P.M., pulling up on the south side near the back porch. Harnish got out of the car first, and as he did, he noticed a long mark on the ground, cutting through the grass and leaves. It looked as though something had been dragged over the earth, he later said. He mentioned the mark to his wife, speculating upon what might have caused it. He thought perhaps someone, for some reason, might have broken down a small tree or carried a branch down from the top of the hill, and he looked around briefly to see if anything else had been disturbed. Nothing had been. With a shrug, he went to the cottage to attend to his chores.

Mrs. Harnish had brought along some bones and scraps of food to put out for the possums that lived in the wood. Now, her interest aroused, she went to look at the track. Later, she said in testimony:

> I investigated the track because it seemed to me, at first appearance, seemed like a track made by a motorcycle, and I thought possibly someone had gone over the hill, because the track went toward the west, and I thought someone might have driven there and gone over the hill. So I investigated it rather carefully then as I noticed the end of the track which disappeared in the leaves right near the brow of the hill, not quite at the brow of the hill. . . . As I looked to see where that mark ended, I—my

attention was called to the fact that it was only a few feet away from the opposite side of the house, the west side of the house, which is much more open than the other side of the house because the hill slants in that direction. . . . There is enough room at the west end of the house to look under the house without stooping greatly, and there is an excavation there in which it is possible to stand up. We had intended to install a heater there just before the war, and this excavation was built for that purpose and never completed, because the heater was not installed. . . . I thought, as I saw how close the mark was to the opening of the excavation that I would look in to see that nothing was disturbed and as I looked in there I noticed, right at the entrance, a footprint of a man's shoe, and that was right at the edge of two long strips of corrugated sheeting that were lying on the ground. . . . I thought everything in there [the excavation] looked natural. There were a few dried leaves around that blow in during the winter. I realized later why I was concerned. It took me two or three days to realize that something in there had been moved. I think that is what attracted my attention. . . .

I lifted up the end of the corrugated iron near the entrance, right where I had seen the footprint, and I saw some objects that made me look much more closely. . . .

The first thing I noticed was a plaid coat. I couldn't say it was a coat, but it looked like the kind of thing we would wear as a lumber jacket. I could see it was red and white and fresh and was not there for rubbish that might have blown in. Therefore, I looked more closely. . . .

I saw next what at first looked like a wig of matted hair. It looked like a wig because the hair was hanging down around a large hole. . . .

Next I noticed what looked like a white blouse and what looked like an arm, and I felt sure, but I could not be sure, of course, that I saw a body.

Mrs. Harnish screamed for her husband, who was up on a ladder putting some morsels of food in a bird-feeding station they maintained. He scrambled down and went running to her. At his approach, she blurted out her grisly discovery. He lifted up the corrugated sheet, peered in, turned to his wife, and nodded. Together they ran for their car, jumped in, and drove a half-mile to the tenant house on their property, where there was a telephone. From there, Harnish called the State Police. They in turn notified city police. Some tipster in the barracks called the office of Lancaster Newspapers, Inc., and the reporters arrived on the scene before the city police.

The State cops came in force—Captain Frank Gleason, Sergeants Vernon Simpson and John Aumon, Corporal James Kane, and Private James Hagerty. Corporal Kane, a trained criminal investigator who was to work on the case throughout, was unofficially in charge of the preliminary investigation. Kane is a burly man, known for his tenacity. Criminal lawyers who have opposed him in court know him as a relentless witness for the prosecution, a hard man to shake in a story, and a by-the-rule-book policeman. He directed that the police cars face the excavation and turn on their lights, for by then it was nearly dark. Soon Commissioner McCartney from the city arrived, accompanied by Captain Kirchner and Detective Frank Matt, who later became Kane's running mate. (There was no question of police jurisdiction, but McCartney quickly assured Gleason of his willingness to have his men co-operate on the case.)

Someone discovered a footprint near the hole, and Corporal Kane ordered a cast made of it. Deputy Coroner Charles P. Stahr arrived, and at four fifty-seven, Corporal Kane raised the corrugated metal. Under them, face down, the head pointing toward the west, was a human body, that of a girl. Corporal Kane directed his detail to take photographs, and when they were finished, the body was turned over.

Dr. Stahr turned his hand torch on the body. Later he said:

> I found the head, as I looked at it with
> my flashlight, a mass of bloody matted hair with
> numbers of leaves and twigs mixed in the hair.
> I found two large wounds in the skull, or in the
> head, one approximately in the right frontal
> region and the other on the posterior side of the
> head involving the left parietal bone.

After his brief preliminary investigation, Dr. Stahr asked the State Police to summon Benjamin Herr, an undertaker, who lives in West Lampeter. Herr and his crew arrived some minutes later, placed the body in a black sack, and removed it to the Lancaster General Hospital. Dr. Stahr's report later said:

> The cause of death was multiple com-
> pound fractures of the skull, involving the right

frontal area and the left parietal area with laceration and maceration of both the hemispheres of the brain. At the site of these wounds there was massive hemorrhage into the brain, into the skull cavity, and massive subarachnoid hemorrhage. Two fragments of the skull were driven into the brain mass. The one from the wound on the left side was lodged almost at the median line dividing the two hemispheres of the brain. The one from the right frontal area was driven into the right hemisphere of the brain.

The body was identified by Donald Mylin, Leroy O'Donel and John Weaver as that of Marian Louise Baker.

At eight one P.M., in the morgue of the Lancaster General Hospital, Dr. George Joseph Heid, Jr., assisted by Dr. R. W. Swan, an intern, performed an autopsy. In court later, Dr. Heid stated:

The face was mostly covered by mud, leaves and twigs so that the features were difficult to recognize. Twigs and leaves were present over the clothing which covered the chest. In addition, the clothing had been turned upward over the chest so that the dirt, leaves and twigs were on the under or next-to-the-skin side of the clothing. There were white pants and they were in the usual position, together with a garter belt which had been pulled downward, especially over the left thigh and to some extent over the right thigh. The straps of the garter belt were attached to sheer stockings, and those straps were intact, so far as I could determine.

40

The feet were shod with dark suede-like shoes. The anterior surface of the thighs were partly covered by a very thin layer of dirt, I believe. . . . The stockings were in place just above the level of the knees, not torn, slightly soiled, with the garter belt attached, elastic attached by metal fasteners. . . . [There was] a large hole on the right side of the forehead, including the hair line. . . . The measurements of that hole in greatest diameter were about two and one-half inches. . . . Also a laceration or tear over the right cheekbone. There was also a tear, or call it laceration of the right eyebrow, in the skin beneath the right eyebrow. . . . Visible on the left side of the neck near the back and about halfway between the hairline and shoulder was a semi-circular abrasion . . . [which] measured about one and one-fourth inches in diameter. There was a marked depression with a slight amount of blood just beneath the skin. . . . Also present was a deep tear in which, on closer inspection, bone could be seen. This tear was immediately behind and just above the left ear. . . . It was later seen that the tear was completely through the left ear into the concavity of the left ear. Also visible over the right shoulder, about halfway between the neck and lateral border or point of the shoulder was a round bruise that measured about one to one and one-fourth inches in diameter. . . . At the back and left side of the head was a large hole in the skin of the scalp, and that hole measured around three inches in diameter. Through this hole, after the hair was parted, a portion of the brain was visible, together with a portion of the thin covering of the brain which is called the dura.

The girl had been murdered with exceptional brutality. There were several other injuries noted on her body. Her right lateral incisor was missing, and in its place was a bloody socket. There were small abrasions of the left hand, and a large bruise which covered much of the back surface of that hand. There were some injuries, small abrasions, to the anterior surface of each thigh, but there were no injuries to the chest, front or back, or to the abdomen, or to the thighs, or to the genitalia.

Doctors Heid and Swan first removed the clothing from the body, handing each article to a policeman who was standing by. Then they took samples of the vegetable matter and soil clinging to the body, and handed them to the officer. Finally they washed the body from head to foot. Dr. Heid then made an incision from the back of the left ear over the top of the head to the back of the right ear, and reflected, or peeled back, the scalp, toward the forehead and toward the neck. This revealed the two holes, one of which, the rear one, was nearly four inches in diameter. Dr. Heid sawed and removed the top of the skull and took out the brain. Much of it was damaged and torn, and when he sectioned it, he found large areas of hemorrhage. Thereafter, he and his assistant opened the abdominal and chest cavities, but found no injuries to the organs. By examining the lungs, he discovered fat emboli. He later said in testimony:

> I must explain that. The under-surface of the skin contains much fat, layers of fat beneath the skin. If traumatic blows are struck, hard,

violent blows on the skin, the fat is broken and injured. In addition, the vessels under the skin are injured and fat droplets from the fat beneath go into the blood vessels. They are driven into the blood vessels. Circulation is such that blood from the skin or any part of the body must eventually reach the lungs. If fat droplets are driven into blood vessels, the capillaries, the finest blood vessels, or the large ones called the veins, those fat droplets eventually reach the lungs in a very short time, perhaps in ten seconds. Those fat droplets are too large to go through the smallest blood vessels in the lungs and there they lodge, so that when the tissue is properly stained (*and examined under a microscope—RG*) the fat is made visible. . . . There were many fat droplets in the vessels of the lungs. . . . That indicated to me that . . . the circulation of the deceased was in action, or . . . the heart was beating while the blows were being struck or for some time after the blows were struck.

Dr. Heid completely dissected the neck. He concluded that there had been no hemorrhage either in the muscles of the neck or the larynx, indicating that the murderer had not exerted sufficient pressure on the victim to produce death by strangulation. He then made a minute examination of the victim's vagina, uterus, cervix, ovaries and oviduct. There was no evidence of violence around the genitalia. He declared later that he could not tell if the victim had had sexual intercourse. He said:

Unless rape is involved with actual damage, you just can't tell whether sexual relations occurred. . . . There is no man who can look at a mature woman and claim she has or has not had intercourse unless there is some injury— forcible intercourse, unless there is some injury. . . . I examined material from the vagina. Nothing indicated. . . . Microscopically I found only squamous epithelial cells. . . . That is, similar to the cells covering the skin, but lining the vagina. There were bacilli germs, but they occur in any woman who is alive, and also may develop after death. . . . I found no spermatozoa. . . . They usually undergo dissolution, or dissolve in no more than six to twelve hours in a dead body.

Dr. Heid's post-mortem pronouncement agreed with Dr. Stahr's. He said:

I feel Marian Baker's death was caused by compound, comminuted and depressed fractures of the skull with tearing and damage to the brain and brain stem.

Corporal Kane had remained at the Harnish cottage after the body was removed by the undertaker, and he and his men began searching the area with flashlights. They did not find a great amount. Near the long drag mark, along the north side of the Harnish driveway, someone picked up a button which later was found to be similar to those on Marian Baker's blouse. Another policeman found an eyelet similar to those on Marian Baker's garter belt. Darkness finally caused the officers to abandon their investigation. There was, however, one other clue. It was a watch in a yellow gold case which Marian Baker wore on her left wrist. The watch had been pulled down from the wrist and was resting in the middle of the lifeless hand. Its crystal was broken. It had stopped at 2:35. With these slim clues to go on, police still felt lucky. During the search for Marian Baker's body, one of the state patrol cars had gone by the Harnish cottage. The officers had seen nothing of note on the grounds, even though one had alighted for a look around. They counted themselves fortunate in the accident of the Harnish couple's having decided to visit their cottage that Saturday before their vacation. "If they'd gone off to Florida *without* going out there," said one officer, "we might *never* have found her." He was reckoning without the murderer, who almost certainly would have led the law to the spot sooner or later.

4

The Search for the Murderer

Three local newspapers are delivered to residents of Lancaster County: the morning *Intelligencer Journal,* the afternoon *New Era,* and the *Sunday News.* All three are products of the same company, Lancaster Newspapers, Inc., which in turn is controlled by two brothers, Colonel J. Hale and John F. Steinman, who also own WGAL, one of two local radio stations, and WGAL-TV, the city's only television station. Politically, the three papers are conservative. The *Intelligencer* leans toward the Democratic party, the *New Era* is unashamedly Republican, and the *Sunday News* is uneasily independent with a distinct rightward list. Nobody is exactly certain how the Steinmans stand politically. Colonel Hale was once a Democratic power, and served in appointive jobs under President Roosevelt. In the last elections he supported Dwight D. Eisenhower, and there is to date no evidence of disenchantment. Whatever their personal politics, the Steinmans give the people of Lancaster three better-than-average small papers. Their front pages are heavily laden

46

with local news. The writing in them is press-association in style and language, which is to say it is adequately communicative. The *Sunday News* broke the story of the finding of Marian Baker's body with a headline that said: MARIAN BAKER FOUND SLAIN. The first edition of the *News* hits the streets shortly after two-thirty A.M. People in Lancaster get out of bed early, even on Sundays. By nine A.M. there was a steady stream of automobiles coursing down Route 222, the main road that leads to the lane that runs by the Harnish property. By eleven A.M. the traffic was as thick as on a holiday in summer. Cars were parked along 222's shoulders for nearly a half-mile. Hordes of people were attempting to go up the lane or across the fields to the cottage. The police finally stationed two patrol cars at the mouth of the lane to keep the curious away. Several people muttered bitter things to the guards. Others tried to take a roundabout way to the property, at the edge of which they were halted and shooed by the police. Many stood at a distance, craning their necks. A few brought binoculars, and one man had a camera with a telephoto lens. Rarely has the power of the Lancaster press been demonstrated more effectively.

The police in Lancaster have taken on some of the methodical coloration of the land they inhabit. Nearly forty of them worked over the Harnish cottage grounds all day Sunday. When they were finished they had to admit that they had uncovered little evidence. Early Sunday morning, Sergeant Simpson came upon a bloodstain about twenty inches in diameter in the leaf-covered ground about sixty-five feet southeast of the cottage. Near this stain he found a tiny patch of hair, later identified as belonging to Marian Baker. Some time after that, Private Paul Schappert found a bone fragment nearly the size of a silver quarter, also near the stain. These three bits of evidence indicated to most of the policemen that the murder had been committed on the grounds. Corporal Kane disagreed. He said the hole in the corpse's head had been so large they probably would have come upon more blood and bone if the girl had been killed near the cottage. He was dead wrong, as he was subsequently informed by the murderer himself.

On Sunday afternoon, Sergeant Aumon happened upon what at first seemed to be the murder weapon. It was a length of pipe, twenty-three inches long and about one and one-quarter inches in diameter, which the Sergeant had noticed as he was scrutinizing that part of Mill Creek which flows near the scene. The pipe was standing approximately upright in the water, one end lodged in mud and the upper part of it resting against a rock. The end protruding above the water contained a deposit which police at first believed to be blood. Since the metal was not rusted, the investigators concluded it had not been long in the creek. Harnish pointed out that plumbers had recently done some work on his property, and there were all sorts of pipe fragments in the vicinity. Nevertheless, Corporal Kane sent the pipe to Harrisburg for further examination and analysis.

None of the policemen, at the end of that day, was willing to say how he thought the crime had been committed, or when, or where. No official statement was given out, but one officer permitted an *Intelligencer Journal* reporter to quote him indirectly and unofficially. The newspaper's report said:

> . . . although the girl's purse . . . and diamond ring, given her by Edgar Rankin, twenty-three-year-old Conestoga R1 fiancé, both were missing, police said they doubted

robbery was the reason for the murder.

Theorizing, one officer expressed the idea the girl went to the spot willingly. Supported by Dr. Stahr's estimate she had been dead from 48 to 72 hours before the discovery of the body, and that she was killed within an hour to an hour and one-half after eating, police said it was possible she was taken there and killed twenty minutes after she was seen leaving the post office.

The time element was borne out by the fact that her wrist watch, which had been broken, had stopped running at 2:35 o'clock. The crystal on the watch had been smashed, possibly from a struggle with the killer.

Explaining his theory the girl voluntarily accompanied the killer to the remote wooded section, the officer said it was highly improbable she would have been forced into an automobile in broad daylight in downtown Lancaster at the time she disappeared.

Because of this, police said, they are almost convinced the killer was at least an acquaintance of Miss Baker. Also, they said, he must have been familiar with the layout of the land in the vicinity of the cottage in order to take her there and leave again, without any known trace of his actions.

It was announced that the police had begun questioning people, but only two were mentioned specifically. One was Edgar Rankin, who was taken to the State Police Barracks on Sunday afternoon shortly before three and released at six. "We questioned him as a routine procedure," said Captain Gleason. "He is definitely not considered a suspect." Gleason later added that the conversation with Rankin had failed to "shed any light on a possible motive." Rankin said, "I have no idea who could have done this terrible thing. We loved each other, and were to be married." The other person questioned was Emory R. Gainer, a thirty-nine-year-old bakery-truck driver, a neighbor of the O'Donels. Gainer appeared voluntarily at the State Police Barracks on Sunday evening; he had heard that they had been seeking him even before the body was found. The police had wanted him because he had been teaching Marian to drive. They had had lessons at regular intervals, he said, and he had taken her to the State Police headquarters some time before for her first test, which she had failed. She had passed the examination on the second try. After questioning him for more than an hour, the police permitted him to go. He gave them no leads, they said.

On Monday morning the investigation switched to the Franklin and Marshall campus. At nine A.M., Dr. Theodore A. Distler, president of the college, called a staff meeting. Among those present were Max E. Hannum, assistant to the president; Dr. Daniel Z. Gibson, dean of the college; Dr. A. G. Breidenstine, dean of men; Donald Mylin; William C. French, alumni secretary; Walter H. Doner, superintendent of college buildings and grounds; Theodore Copeland, assistant dean of students; Richard V. Showers, director of placement; and Officers Davis, Aumon, Haggerty, Kane and Matt.

Dr. Distler issued a public statement which said:

The college community is deeply shocked
and saddened at the death of Marian Louise

Baker, who has served the college faithfully and well since 1946.

The college desires to lend all assistance in the solution of this terrible crime and will co-operate with the proper authorities in every possible way.

By way of substantiating the latter claim, Dean Breidenstine then laid the identity of the murderer in the laps of the officers. He said that he had been approached two days before by a student, the son of an undertaker. The boy was badly frightened. Another student had accosted him and asked how long it ordinarily would take a human body to decompose. Upon questioning, the undertaker's son had told Dean Breidenstine the name of the other student. The Dean gave this name to the police. He added that he had seen the student on the campus, and that he had a scar on one of his cheeks. It looked like he might have been scratched, the Dean said.

The officers gravely wrote the information down but did not immediately act upon it for reasons which they have not disclosed. One theory advanced by reporters is that preliminary questioning of individuals who had been close to Marian Baker had given the police a suspect of their own. The man was never mentioned in public, and today the police might deny that they had marked him, but there are two witnesses who assert that the investigation centered about him for some time. He was Donald Mylin. There were three reasons which put him into the police's minds. First, there was his fondness for Marian Baker. Second, he was unable to furnish a consistent alibi for the afternoon on which she disappeared. Initially, he said he had refereed a swimming meet; the reporters found that there had been no meet that day. Then Mylin said he had taken his brother to the railroad station. The reporters found that if he had done so, he still would have had time to take Marian Baker out and kill her before getting back to his office. The police were all but set to arrest him, but John Milton Ranck, the District Attorney, admonished them to hold off. Later two reporters visited Mylin's summer cottage near Conestoga. There they found two exciting bits of evidence. One was a note that said "Send help." (They later concluded that it had been left by children playing cops-and-robbers in the vicinity.) Another was a series of spots on the rear steps. They decided the spots were dried blood. It was later ascertained that Mylin had been doing some painting. The reporters, Glenn C. Abel and Marvin Miller, dashed back to report their findings to the police, but by that time—Wednesday afternoon—the murderer had been arrested. Mylin was not aware that he was under suspicion; or, if he was, he did not show it. He evidently attributed the police's exhaustive questioning to his position as Marian's superior.

It may be that police had the murderer under close surveillance throughout the period that elapsed before his arrest. This seems unlikely, for at least one of his curious actions should have aroused their interest. The same crowd that had gathered around the Harnish property on Sunday began appearing each night at the Lancaster Newspapers office to grab the first edition of the *Intelligencer Journal,* which comes off the presses between two and two thirty A.M. The murderer was in that group each night. He was later identified by Mrs. Elizabeth Baker, the night telephone operator. She told reporters, "He would walk into the first floor of the building where I sat at the switchboard and ask if the papers were off the press yet. When they were available he would buy one, but never look at it while he was still in the building. When they were not off the press he would leave, and return later to make the purchase. He never showed any outward signs of emotion that aroused my suspicion."

In other respects the police were admirably—if perhaps a trifle pointlessly—efficient. On Monday they began checking lists of known sex offenders. At Franklin and Marshall they began making up and examining lists of students and employees. They put together lists of Marian Baker's acquaintances, of students who owned automobiles, and one of students who had been off the campus on Tuesday afternoon. There was one other list, said to be a "hot" one, which they would not describe. (They still will not.) The murderer's name, it later was found, was on every one of these lists, but this fact apparently escaped the officers.

Certain officers, while their cohorts were making up and checking the lists, went to Conestoga and began interrogating every person known to have known Marian. Poor Rankin again was subjected to a long session, and so were his parents, Mr. and Mrs. Maris Rankin, and his sisters. The police broadcast a plea to local garagemen, asking them to report any cars with stained upholstery. They asked laundries to report bloodstained clothing, and they requested stores to carefully examine the cars of people buying new slip covers.

That morning's edition of the *Intelligencer Journal* carried an editorial that said:

THE WORST HAS COME TO PASS

The worst has come to pass.

As had been feared by many, Marian Baker was murdered; beaten to death by someone she met as she did an errand in the downtown section of the city Tuesday afternoon.

The community is shocked, and well it might be.

For it is, undoubtedly, the worst crime of its kind ever committed around here.

It calls for an immediate solution because, whatever the motive, it gives a feeling of insecurity to all women.

Obviously, its solution will test the best brains in crime detection, and the State should put every available investigator on the case.

Twenty-four hours have already elapsed since the body was found, without a significant development.

Actually five days have elapsed since the crime was committed, without a significant development.

And every minute the trail grows colder.

It is unthinkable that the crime should not be solved. But that has happened before. And it could happen again. But it must not happen in this case, and that is why we are asking an all-out effort by every investigator at the State's command.

But, as we have pointed out time and again, crime detection calls for the co-operation of the citizens.

There may be, somewhere in the city or county, some citizen with some information concerning the case which would be of great value to the investigators. If there is someone with information, he, or she, should not attempt to evaluate it. That should be left up to the investigators.

54

Many criminal cases have been solved by some seemingly meagre bit of information from some alert citizen. It is possible that such could be the case in this investigation.

So we ask the public to co-operate with the police in solving this crime.

Monday night, Captain Gleason had to tell the reporters, "There's nothing new—we wish we had something."

On Tuesday morning the police learned two facts. Preliminary, inconclusive reports from the laboratory all but proved that the length of pipe was not the murder weapon, for the substance inside it was not blood. Then an expert from Hamilton Watch Company, Harold Anderson, who had been examining the watch found on Marian's wrist, aided in ascertaining the time of her death. He said that the watch had a running-time of thirty-five hours when wound, and that its balance wheel, pivot staff, and crystal evidently had been broken by a sharp blow at two thirty-five. Mrs. Weaver had previously told police that Marian had been in the habit of winding her watch every morning when she awakened, usually around seven or seven thirty. The time of her death thus was fixed at about two thirty-five P.M. the preceding Tuesday. An analysis of the contents of her stomach, which showed that she had eaten about two hours before her death, also fixed the time. The analysis was made by two Philadelphia city police chemists; it showed that she had eaten a tangerine or orange, lima beans, beets, potatoes, and a small amount of a green leafy vegetable. That coincided with the college cafeteria's menu on the day of her disappearance.

A few police officers in plain clothes went out to Conestoga to Marian Baker's funeral on Tuesday morning, hoping they might see some suspicious behavior on the part of someone in the crowd. They saw nothing except excessive grief, one of the few legitimate and publicly acceptable emotions in the Lancaster County lexicon. The services were held at the Oscar H. Gundel Funeral Home. The evening before, a viewing had been held for members of the immediate family and close friends. The stiff, mutilated body lay clad in a long-sleeved pink satin gown. The casket was two-toned bronze. Reverend William Kutz, of the Conestoga Evangelical and Reformed Church, conducted the services, assisted by Dr. John B. Noss, head of the Department of Philosophy at Franklin and Marshall. There were approximately one hundred people present, and there were, perhaps, more flowers than Marian might have received if she had not been murdered. The crew who worked with O'Donel at Conestoga sent a spray, and so did her co-workers at the college. So did the Conestoga baseball club. Mrs. Bruce Britcher, mother of the deceased, arrived at the last minute with her husband. She bore up well. Mrs. Leroy O'Donel, on the other hand, appeared on the verge of collapse. O'Donel's face was white, and he was doing a valiant job of keeping himself under control. The service lasted thirty minutes, after which the pallbearers—Elmer Huber, Maris Shaub, Edward Weaver and Robert Kreiter, all old friends of Marian—carried the casket to the hearse, which made the dismal journey to New Bloomfield followed by two station wagons (lent by the college) full of flowers, and cars carrying approximately fifty mourners. The procession was also followed by the plainclothesmen, who mingled with the crowd at the cemetery. Edgar Rankin and his brother, Raymond, helped carry Marian Baker's coffin from hearse to grave. When it was lowered, Edgar Rankin turned his back. He was sobbing, and his shoulders shook.

That same day, the police announced they were "starting from scratch." By then there were twenty detectives, city and state, working full time on the case. A total of fifteen hundred man-hours of work had been expended since Saturday. The college authorities, particularly Dean Breidenstine, were unable to understand why some of these man-hours had not been expended in interrogating the most likely suspect. The police did not account for their ways. That evening, Captain Gleason said, "Things look brighter than they have looked for twenty-four hours." Again he did not elaborate.

The city, by this time, was thoroughly aroused. More than three hundred telephone calls came into the city and state headquarters. The police checked each one, and found nothing. Someone reported that there was a student who had dated Marian Baker two or three times during a spat she had had with Rankin. It was learned that he had moved to Florida some time before, and had not left that state. An eight-year-old girl who lived on Reynolds Avenue reported that she had seen Marian Baker get into a car and drive off with a man the preceding week. The police checked her story and concluded she was mistaken.

Tuesday night, Garden Spot Post No. 1690, Veterans of Foreign Wars, met and offered a resolution and a reward of twenty-five dollars for the arrest of the killer. Post Commander Thomas W. Lainhoff said, in a prepared statement:

"The efforts of state and local police have not been sufficient to track down the ruthless fiend who murdered Miss Baker. The break must come from some member of our community who, willing or not, holds some small scrap of information that may be just the thing needed to crack this case."

On Wednesday morning, one officer said, "When a break comes, it will come fast." He would say nothing more. He did not have to; the break came perhaps more swiftly than he had anticipated.

The murderer confessed that afternoon.

5

The Murderer

People who knew Edward Lester Gibbs had difficulty believing, at first, that he was the murderer of Marian Louise Baker. It did not seem possible that he could have done it. His home town, Pitman, New Jersey, looks as though it would be the last place in the world to produce an Edward Gibbs.

Pitman is a quiet borough of about seven thousand people located eight miles due south of Camden. It is much younger than Lancaster, but its placidity and smallness make it seem older. The old trees form leafy arches over the streets, and the white frame houses sit calmly behind them, giving the town an air of comfortable well-being, perhaps even of smugness. The Pitman slogan is "Everybody likes Pitman." Only Broadway, the main thoroughfare, makes a gesture to commerce, and that for no more than three blocks of little stores and shops. These establishments are huddled together as though enjoying mutual protection and prosperity, their faded green and brown and weathered white fronts marred here and there by an occasional red and blue neon sign. Pitman has no industry. The day laborers go to the Owens-Illinois works at Glassboro, to the Radio Corporation of America plant in Camden, or to the huge cat-cracker put up by The Texas Company at near-by Eagle Point. White-collar workers commute to Philadelphia and Camden. "Pitman is a bedroom town," one of its old residents has said. "Men come home at nights to sleep and go away to work in the mornings." The average income in Pitman is high, and so is the tax rate. There is only one hotel, and the railroad stationmaster goes to work only about nine times a day, whenever a West Jersey and Seashore line train stops. The town is governed by a mayor and council, but the only full-time salaried elective officer is the tax collector. The people are almost unanimously Republican. There are six full-time policemen and three volunteer fire companies. None of these officers have much to do, for the town is tranquil to the point of dullness. No one can remember a murder ever having been committed in Pitman. There is one movie theater and a pool parlor, but there are no saloons or beer joints. This is directly attributable to the Methodists, who have always run Pitman. Around 1871, a group of Methodist ministers began holding a summer camp meeting on grounds now occupied by the town. They held it regularly each summer, and presently built a pavilion for their services. As time went on, streets were laid out around this pavilion like spokes in a wheel, and little frame cottages were erected along them. Eventually some of the older campers began living in these cottages the year around. Today the camp meetings are still held each summer, but the sessions have been considerably shortened; they begin on one Sunday, run through the next, and end on a third. The cottages today are almost all permanent homes.

Pitman began to grow out from the wheel in the early 1900's, but the Methodists retained a firm grip on local mores. For a long time, no automobiles were allowed within Pitman's limits on the Sabbath. The W.C.T.U. has always been strong, and some years ago, when an enterprising tavernkeeper put up a place outside the town, the good ladies waged an almost-successful fight to restrain him. He won out, and his place now mocks them with a lively custom drawn mainly from Pitman younger people and backsliders. People in near-by communities have called Pitman "The dry town with a bar in every basement." Though the Methodists' power has been somewhat challenged in recent years by the Presbyterians, and also by the Roman Catholics, who built a Pitman church in 1950, they have managed to remain supreme.

The crime of Edward Gibbs would have shocked any community. It was doubly shocking to Pitman, first because Gibbs was popularly regarded, with notable exceptions, as something of a model young man, and second because he came from a family that had been active and influential in the town, if not, perhaps, as wealthy as the newspapers indicated. The Gibbs name is an old and respected name in South Jersey. Edward's father, J. Lester Gibbs, came originally from South Camden, in company with an older brother, Roy C., and a younger one, Walter. Roy C. is regarded in Pitman as one of the town's wealthier men; a friend of his has said, "Roy swings a lot of weight in this state." Walter Gibbs, until the 1953 elections, served three terms as Mayor of Pitman. It is common gossip in the town that Roy C. put up the money for Edward's defense, for most people regard J. Lester as the least prosperous of the trio. He was a shipping and traffic manager throughout most of his working career in the

61

Dunne Linoleum Company, a Camden floor-covering concern with which all three brothers were associated, Roy C. as the partner of a man from New York. The company evidently was at one time fairly successful and profitable in proportion to its size. It is no longer in existence. Edward Gibbs was the only male issue of the three Gibbs brothers, and the sole child of his father and the former Florence Saqui, who came from near-by Clayton. There is no evidence of any insanity on the Gibbs side of the family. At Gibbs' trial, his defense attorney produced references to two minor instances of instability on the Saqui side. Dr. Edward A. Strecker, the psychiatrist called as defense witness, testified in regard to them. Gibbs' maternal great-grandmother, Elizabeth Saqui, was confined to the Cumberland County, New Jersey, hospital at Bridgeton from about 1927 to 1940, when she died. Her particular affliction was a fear of electricity in any shape or form; she became disturbed if light was turned on her. Ethelbert Saqui, a maternal uncle of Gibbs, was in the Philadelphia General Hospital, psychopathic department, some time before Christmas 1949, for mental disturbances. He received shock treatments there. Dr. Strecker testified, "I have some idea, but I am not sure, it was connected with alcoholism."

Pitman has no hospital of its own. Parents who want their children to be born away from home, in a hospital, must go to Woodbury, a town fourteen or fifteen miles away. Edward Lester Gibbs was born in the Woodbury Hospital at twelve eighteen A.M. on December 1, 1924. He was delivered by Dr. J. Harris Underwood, of Woodbury. It was an occiput forceps delivery, and the baby sustained some superficial lacerations of the lips from the forceps. He was administered artificial respiration for

62

several minutes after his birth, which had occurred in prolonged labor. He did not nurse readily for the first three
or four days; after that, he nursed very well. His birth was
a signal for rejoicing among the three Gibbs brothers; one
Pitman citizen remembers that the uncles seemed as
pleased as the father himself.

In a letter to Gibbs' defense attorney written February 28, 1950, Dr. Edward A. Strecker stated:

> Edward Lester Gibbs . . . was very def-
> initely spoiled by his parents and was inade-
> quately prepared to meet the stresses of every-
> day life. . . . His mother . . . was definitely
> an emotionally possessive parent. . . . He
> never received adequate preparation and train-
> ing for leading a reasonably satisfactory per-
> sonal and social adult life.

Those who knew Gibbs and his parents from the
time of his birth testify that this is cautious understate-
ment. The first word used to describe Mrs. Florence
Gibbs is invariably "high-strung." She was once confined
to bed for some time with a "nervous breakdown." Her
husband has been described by acquaintances as a mild-
mannered, inoffensive, almost ineffectual man, who must
have been unaware of, or unable to do anything about,
his wife's extremely protective attitude toward their son.
A neighbor remembers that when little Eddie, as he was
always called, was put out to play in the yard behind the
house, Mrs. Gibbs either poked her head out the door or
ran outside every five or ten minutes to have a look at
him. The Gibbs house is on a street that runs parallel to
Broadway, one block below. Its address is 48 North Oak

Avenue, and that street is as barren of traffic as any Pitman thoroughfare during the daytime hours, for most of Pitman's men drive their automobiles off to work in the mornings. A close boyhood companion of Gibbs recalls that whenever the two of them went on a hike, or were going out to play ball, "Mrs. Gibbs told Eddie to be careful and not to get hurt, over and over. She told him to be careful about a hundred times every time."

The mother's disposition affixed itself to the boy. One of Edward Gibbs' elementary-school teachers, a lady who has seen a twenty-year panorama of children, recalls him as one of the most nervous ever to sit in her room. He also impressed a high-school teacher that way. "I thought he was neurotic—that's the only word," this lady, an English teacher in Pitman High, has said. "He used to be up and down in his seat a half-dozen times in every class period. I think he wanted to pay attention, but he was too nervous. He had one distasteful nervous habit—he used to wipe his nose, quickly, smearing his hand across his face. It annoyed me. Yet I liked him. He was in many ways a likable boy. I think he could have worked a little harder, but he was too nervous." According to Henry Cooper, principal of Pitman High, Gibbs' I.Q. was 119–120. Yet Cooper's records show him graduating seventy-eighth in a class of seventy-eight. He was fondest of history, but never made high marks, and least fond of English, which he failed once. In a school questionnaire prepared by the Guidance Department, he reported that he spent one hour per night on homework, and that Latin occupied most of his time. Each year, Pitman High students are ranked by their teachers on initiative, neatness, accuracy, industry, punctuality and co-operation. Ten is a perfect score. For his senior year, Gibbs' rating-sheet was as follows:

Initiative	7-8-6-5-7
Neatness	6-6-8-6-7
Accuracy	5-5-6-6-8
Industry	5-7-6-5-7
Punctuality	7-8-6-6-8
Co-operation	9-9-6-5-9

Although Gibbs was never particularly strong, and was always slightly underweight while in school, he enjoyed fairly good health. In 1937, in another questionnaire, he wrote that he had been absent 20 times throughout his school life for "sickness." He also wrote that he went to bed each night at eight thirty and arose at eight A.M. As a child he had whooping cough and measles, but escaped diphtheria and scarlet fever in company with most children of his generation. One teacher recalls that he once had several fingers broken, but cannot remember how it happened. His tonsils were removed, but the operation did not cure his early-set habit of breathing through his mouth. Dr. Strecker, commenting on this later, wrote: ". . . the nasal septum shows some angulation toward the right with spur formation on the right side. . . . Gibbs has had sinus difficulty for years . . . it has been much worse within the past year with rather persistent headache." Gibbs' upper incisors always protruded slightly, but not unattractively. His lips were invariably moist. A girl who knew him at Franklin and Marshall has said of him: "His mouth, as I remember him, was never closed. It looked almost *slobberish* at times." As a small boy and high school student, Gibbs was quite personable. He had dark hair, a strong nose, and an ingratiating smile. Later, when he returned from the service, the fragile features of childhood were hardened somewhat; and still later, before the time of his crime, he had gained weight. He stood five feet, eight and one half inches and weighed 148. One of the last pictures taken of him shows his face full, and his neck somewhat puffed beneath the jaws.

While attending Pitman High, Gibbs suffered a head injury, which later was considered significant enough to be introduced into testimony at his trial. In court, he described it by saying:

> . . . I was playing basketball with a local team and we had been to a tournament, and there were 2 cars. On the way home I was in the first car. I got out to tell the fellows in the second car we were going to get something to eat, and when I was out of the first car the fellow started to drive away. I thought he was just kidding, so I jumped on the running board—it was a 1939 Willys-Knight with a very small running board—when he shifted into second, I knew he wasn't kidding and I stepped off and I was thrown.
>
> Q—How fast was he going, approximately, when you stepped off?
>
> A—He said 30 to 35 miles per hour.
>
> Q—What happened to you?
>
> A—I took a complete flip and was knocked unconscious.
>
> Q—Did you find out later how long you were unconscious?
>
> A—Approximately 45 minutes.
>
> Q—What did you suffer?
>
> A—I had a severe blow to my head, and my shoulders and my arms.

Commenting on this on the witness stand, Dr. Strecker said:

. . . [it] may have been serious. It was diagnosed as concussion. . . . He was at first not unconscious—and I mention this because I think it makes it perhaps all the more important—then unconsciousness came on gradually. It sometimes comes on with bleeding within the skull. I don't know whether that was so or not, but he did become unconscious and was taken to the hospital under the care of a doctor, and was unconscious, I am told, for approximately 35 minutes. The important part of that diagnosis was the concussion of the brain.

In telling Dr. Strecker of his schooldays in Pitman, Gibbs said, "I was a big frog in a little pond." It was true, despite his spidery build. Perhaps because he was secretly a physical coward and needed to prove himself, perhaps because he was seeking from the outside world the attention and applause and approval he received so copiously at home—whatever the reason, he excelled in sports as few students have in the entire history of Pitman High. He won varsity letters in football, basketball, baseball and track, and was given a special award for athletic achievement at his graduation exercises. He always played hard. "We knew he wasn't yellow," Principal Cooper has said. The captain of the Pitman Panthers basketball team during Gibbs' senior year, has added: "He gave his all when he played." Gibbs was responsible for several spectacular and unexpected feats by Pitman teams. Woodbury High has always defeated Pitman in football. During one game with Woodbury, Gibbs ran seventy yards for a touchdown that made the final score 7–6; although Woodbury had a one-point margin, it was the closest Pitman ever came to winning, and was regarded as a moral victory. In Gibbs' senior year, 1942–43, Pitman football and basketball teams won the Tri-county championships (the Tri-county was once composed of teams from Gloucester, Salem and Camden counties; Camden later dropped out of the conference, but the name has remained). In basketball, Gibbs was a dead shot when he was on his game; the captain would instruct the other players to feed him the ball. Other times, when Gibbs was not in perfect form, the ball was kept away from him. Annoyed, Gibbs would demand the ball in time-out arguments. There was much dissension on the basketball team that season—so much, in fact, that the captain later could not understand how his squad managed to win the cup. Much of the contention was caused by a running argument between Gibbs and a teammate, who once had been close friends. The two were competing for a guard position. They competed so earnestly that their friendship suffered, and a coolness developed between their families. Gibbs' mother and father were his most avid fans. They went to every contest in which he participated, even those with schools miles away from Pitman. One teammate remembers that either J. Lester Gibbs or his wife always carried the boy's gym bag, and they cheered him immoderately from the stands. "If my dad and mother had ever behaved like that, it would have embarrassed hell out of me," one basketball player later said. Playing in a basketball game with Clayton High, Gibbs was dribbling down the floor swiftly toward a guard named LaVoula, a boy who was big for his age. LaVoula would give no ground, and they collided. Gibbs went down, but was on his feet belligerently in an instant. From the bleachers, his mother cried, "Sock 'im, Eddie!" in a voice that could be heard throughout the gym. The crowd laughed. From then on, some of Gibbs' friends kidded him by calling him "Sock 'im,

Eddie." It was in his conduct in sports events that Gibbs first began to exhibit the quick temper that many of his Pitman friends have called his most outstanding characteristic. He was a poor loser. Once, after a defeat by a narrow margin, two of his friends found him in the dressing room in an uncontrollable rage, beating his fists against the row of metal lockers. Another time, the track team was preparing to go to Philadelphia to compete in the annual Penn Relays. The senior class trip to Washington was scheduled for two days prior to the track meet, and the coach announced beforehand that seniors who went on the trip would not be permitted to participate in the races. He said he wanted every runner to be in perfect condition. Gibbs called the team's captain aside and asked him what he planned to do. "I'm giving up the trip," the captain said. "I won't give it up," Gibbs said. "I want to have some fun in Washington." The senior class returned from Washington on Friday afternoon. Saturday morning, as the Relays team was preparing to leave, Gibbs arrived at the gym, bag in hand, ready to go. "I feel fine," he said. "I'm in good shape." The coach said, "Nothing doing, Eddie. You knew what the deal was." According to an eyewitness, "Gibbs argued with him. He got red-eyed. He raised his voice. The coach stood firm, and the team left without Gibbs. We heard from one of the other guys that Eddie went down to the locker room and sat there bawling for about an hour." The team won its event in the relays. "That seemed to hurt him twice as much—that we'd won it without him, that we hadn't needed him," one runner has recalled. Although he became emotional in games, Gibbs never went to pieces under pressure; but one or two times he got so keyed up that the captain called time to cool him off. His releases came mainly after the games were over, when he would break into tears or indulge in excesses of hilarity. "Eddie couldn't ever seem to play it cool," a friend has commented. He could not hold his temper in an argument, either; Lewis Preston Brooks, known in Pitman as Pres, the proprietor of a gas station in which Gibbs worked in his spare time, has said, "He was a very excitable kid. In any discussion he'd try to shout you down instead of reasoning." Others attest that Gibbs' conduct in an argument was more vocal than logical. Yet Brooks contends, "Gibbs came from as fine a pair of people as you'd want to find anywhere. They raised the kid right, as good as you could want. The parents may have shown him a little too much devotion, but hell, that may have been natural. I have a kid here. He plays football, and I always get a little exuberated about him myself. It's a natural thing." None of the athletes who witnessed Gibbs' locker-room temper tantrums felt them worth mentioning to the faculty or to older people, apparently. Principal Cooper regrets this, and has brooded over it a good deal. "If I'd heard of that temper at the time," he says, "I'd have gone up to the kid and given him a good kick in the rear, just to see what he'd have done. Then, if he'd lost his temper like that, I'd have tried to find out why . . . tried to get him some help." Cooper, in outlining his main impressions of Gibbs as a student, continues, "If you put authority on the kid, he would take that. He was never a discipline problem, ever. He wanted to be well thought of. He was mannerly, although his table manners were bad . . . he had a gross manner of eating that to me indicated how self-centered he was. But he always sought to be socially acceptable."

Gibbs' athletic prowess was never completely satisfying to him. He tried to be the biggest man in school in other ways. He was the flashiest dresser, one friend remembers: "His sports jackets and ties were always louder than anybody else's." Gibbs' graduation picture shows him wearing a loud plaid sport jacket. His voice was as loud as his clothes were. *Talisman,* the senior class yearbook at Pitman High, contains a number of entries which throw some light on what Gibbs' contemporaries thought of him. The caption under his picture is: "Let the dance go on; let joy be unrestrained." In the class prophecy, the entry is as follows: "Edward Gibbs . . . Especially garrulous . . . Teacher of dancing to Arthur Murray." In the class will:

"Ed Gibbs' arguing to Carl Lemmer."

Nobody who knew Gibbs in those days recalls him as being much of a hand with the girls, but everyone remembers that he liked to give the impression that he was. Comparatively speaking, he was a big spender. "He always had an extra five or so on a date," one friend remembers. "I think he got it from one of his uncles; when we would go out on double dates, he'd sometimes stop off at one of the uncles' houses 'Just to say hello' before picking up his girl. I think the uncle would slip him a five-spot then." Gibbs had no regular girl in high school; he went around with a group of three or four, most often on double dates with his friends. He drove his father's car, a Ford. "To tell the truth, I sort of hated to go out on a double date with him," one of his schooldays companions has said. "He always had more cash, and you were afraid he'd go somewhere where you'd have to blow a five-dollar bill. Hell, a *dollar* bill was a lot of money to a high-school kid in those days. Yet he was generous. If he knew you were short, he'd help you out. He insisted on it. And he was generous in other ways. I remember a couple of times when he was driving the car on a double date, my girl lived out in the country. He'd take me out there and drop me off at her house, then take his girl home, then come back and pick me up about an hour and a half later. He seemed glad to do it; willing, maybe even anxious to do that favor." Gibbs particularly liked to be seen in Pitman with some girl from out of town, preferably a strikingly pretty one. Once his cousin Virginia, who attended Penn Hall, a private school for girls, brought some of her classmates to Pitman for the weekend. Gibbs was excited for days ahead of time. He made elaborate arrangements for an evening's party consisting of some of the basketball players and the out-of-town girls. "He always liked to make a big time of things, to arrange a party and to be the center of fun," Alexander Denmead has said. After dates, Gibbs liked to sit around with his friends and discuss the girls they'd taken out. "To a fellow like me, who never made out, he liked to pretend that he *always* made out," one friend says. "If a girl turned him down, though, he never hesitated to do something to run her down the creek. He would even say something nasty about her to get even; he'd say she *let* him, or something, or gave the idea that she had. He was sort of spiteful that way." One girl who dated him has said, "Whenever you went out with Eddie, it was a wrestling match." Gibbs was a virgin until some time after he went in the Army. He never spoke truthfully of his sexual experiences until after his arrest, when he discussed them, in part, with Dr. Strecker. In a letter, Dr. Strecker later said:

> The pattern of his sex life was, in my opinion, definitely abnormal. In his boyhood he never masturbated. I quite believe the statement since Mr. Gibbs is sufficiently well-informed to know that there is nothing unusual or abnormal in a certain amount of masturbation in boyhood, and in fact it occurs in an overwhelmingly

large percentage of boys at some stage of their development. During his high school years, and before, Gibbs had no sex relationships of any kind. In fact he had no sex relationships until he was over-seas with the Army in Italy. He was then placed in a situation where it was almost impossible for him to escape going with a group of boys to a house of prostitution. He had pretended with the soldiers he knew that he was sexually sophisticated and experienced. In this house of prostitution, a prostitute was assigned to him who was pregnant. He could not have relationship with her. Some weeks later, he was again placed in the same position and went to a house of prostitution with four other soldiers. There was only one prostitute available, and the five men drew lots as to the order in which they would have sex relationship with this prostitute. He was number three. When he entered the girl's room, she told him that she was menstruating, but she offered to perform an abnormal sex act for him. This filled him with disgust and repugnance, and he left her presence. Gibbs' first sex relationship was early in 1944 in Italy with a prostitute. Gibbs had three sex relationships before his marriage.

While at Pitman High, Gibbs supplemented the money from his parents and uncles by taking various odd jobs. He worked in Brooks' gas station; he set up pins in a bowling alley; he helped out in the floor covering company in Camden. He graduated in 1943, and went immediately into the service. This part of his career was covered in testimony as follows:

Q— . . . [you said] you were inducted into the Army the day after graduation. What branch of the Army did you enlist in?

A—I enlisted in the Army Air Corps for pilot training. I had a serial number, induction serial number, for the simple reason you had to be a volunteer, to be drawn out, in order to get in the Army.

Q—Where were you sent?

A—Keesler Field, Biloxi, Mississippi.

*

Q—How long were you there?

A—Approximately 3 weeks.

Q—And from there, where were you assigned?

A—Birmingham Southern College, Birmingham, Alabama.

Q—How long were you there?

A—Approximately 5 months.

Q—Were you able to qualify as a pilot?

A—At that phase, yes. I graduated.

Q—Did you subsequently qualify?

A—No, sir, I didn't.

Q—What happened? Did you flunk, or ——?

A—The phase at Birmingham Southern College I passed and was sent on to the next step which was Nashville, Tennessee, for classification, and we were given certain tests, both mental and physical, and through these tests I was declared ineligible to continue my pilot training.

Q—How did that affect you?

A—I was very much broken up about it.

Q—Then where were you sent?

A—Scott Field, Illinois.

Q—What did you do there?

A—I was sent into radio work—code.

Q—Did you complete that work?

A—No, I didn't. The constant code, constant taking of code, on my head, was too much. I couldn't stand it; too much pressure.

(Gibbs was left-handed. His parents made him learn to write with his right hand, and attempted to get him to eat with it, but he remained left-handed in most other activities. He was a southpaw in baseball, and he threw forward passes with his left hand in football games. Dr. Baldwin L. Keyes, the prosecution's psychiatrist witness, later suggested that he may have flunked out in his Army tests because of his left-handedness.)

The testimony continued:

Q—Then where did you go?

A—I was put on overseas shipment, went overseas and was sent to Italy.

Q—What work did you do in Italy?

A—I was a control tower operator, first operator, Control operator, 98th Bomber Group, 15th Air Force.

Q—What were your duties?

A—The take off and landing and safety provisions of all ships on our field.

Q—You mean you had the responsibility of getting the ships off the ground and bringing them in?

A—Yes, sir, it was wholly in my hands.

Q—What experience did you have there?

A—Of course, in combat we had quite a few airplanes crack up, had ships come back low in gas, the hydraulic systems shot out, no brakes, flat tires, which you knew would always incur a crash, wounded men on board. We also had Italian ships flying off our field; they were under British control, flying into Yugoslavia dropping supplies to Marshal Tito. At that time we had no radio contact with them and they would persist in going out on the runways, landing as they pleased.

Q—What about the number of crashes? Did you see them?

A—Yes, when we were preparing to cover the invasion of Southern France, it gave a lot of night transition work which the pilots weren't used to. We were practicing——

Q—Did you have any experience then?

A—They were practicing, and it was my habit that when I couldn't see the ship clear the runway because of darkness, I would have the ship call back as soon as it cleared the runway and tell the control tower he was in flight so that I knew it was perfectly safe to send the next ship on the runway. This one night I was on night transition and a ship asked for clearance and I gave it to him. He started down the runway, took off, called the control tower by name, "Curry Control. This is Red Kate-Katey. I am air borne," and at that instant he blew up and his hands must still have been on the mike button pressing down because the awfullest scream, unearthly scream you ever heard in your lifetime came across.

Q—Later on did you imagine you heard that scream?

A—Not after I got back from the service, but for a few weeks afterward I could still hear it.

Q—You then finished your tower duty in Italy?

A—That is right.

Q—How long were you in the service, altogether?

A—28 months.

Q—And you came back to this country when?

A—In May of 1944.

Q—Bound where?

A—We were bound to go to Japan . . . pick up a B-29, and go direct to Japan.

Q—Now, on your re-assignment, where were you sent?

A—I was sent to Fairmount, Nebraska.

Q—And subsequently, where else?

A—El Pason, Bates Field, El Paso; then to Demming, New Mexico on detached service, put in charge of a bomb range control tower.

While in New Mexico, Gibbs suffered a head injury which Dr. Strecker later considered of sufficient note to include mention of it in his testimony. Gibbs described it in court as follows:

A—One evening while I was on leave in town I had a date with a girl. I walked outside of town, had taken her home, and around mid-night, as the taxi and bus service in the small town was very inadequate, as was the housing conditions——

Q—Just tell us what happened.

A—Returning home to this through desert area, through the main part of town, I was struck by an instrument, I don't know what kind, knocked unconscious and robbed.

Q—Do you know how long you were unconscious?

A—No, sir, I have no idea.

Q—Were you hospitalized?

A—No, sir, I wasn't.

Another of Gibbs' service experiences may have been tied directly to his lifelong desire to be spectacular, to become the cynosure of any group to which he happened to belong. His attorney questioned him in court as follows:

Q—Did you have a tank or gas truck catch fire?

A—Yes, sir, one day—working with the control tower we were very closely associated with the crew of the fire fighting outfit and the wrecking crews on wrecks because we ate together and we had——

Q—What happened?

A—There was a 6 x 6 carry-all that the army used and a 100 octane gas truck backed together, a truck loaded with 100 octane gas, and they were on fire. In this area there was a large amount of B-24's and bombs the armament men were getting prepared to load for the next day's missions, and everybody was afraid to go near the fire for we didn't know quite when the truck might go up because of the gasoline on board. I don't know what made me do it, but I thought——

Q—Just what did you do?

A—I went out to the tractor trailer which was loaded with gasoline, climbed in the cab, threw the switch, shoved it into gear and drove it away from the 6 x 6 out into the infield and the fire company followed me and put it out, and that was all.

Q—What was your reaction?

A—After it was all finished and I got out of it I was shaking like a leaf, very nervous, and I don't know what made me do it. It was just an impulse. Afterwards I realized how close danger was.

Gibbs did not mention in testimony that he had had to make a major adjustment in his eating habits when he first went into the service. He described this to Dr. Keyes, who later wrote:

. . . The contrast [with civilian life] was very difficult. He explains that he disliked the food and the noisy mess halls, so that his family sent him food and money to buy meals outside. This indulgence, he realizes, made it more difficult for him to adjust . . .

Gibbs was mustered out of the Army on August 13, 1945. He went immediately to Pitman and, after a short rest, went to work, first in Brooks' gas station, and later in a station in Atlantic City. Almost as soon as he arrived home he and his parents began discussing the problem of whether or not he should go to college. He did not want to go; he wanted to begin working in a job that interested him—although he had not yet decided what that job might be. His parents were insistent. Gibbs later told both Dr. Strecker and Dr. Keyes that his father seemed to feel that going to college was "the thing to do." The uncles were anxious for him to get a degree, too. It was decided that he would elect courses in Business Administration. He had heard that Franklin and Marshall College was sound in this field, and accordingly wrote a letter to the Registrar in September, 1945. The letter said, in part:

> Please state the tuition and other expenses separate from the board, as I am sure that is not included in the tuition, as my tuition will be paid through the G.I. bill of rights. Also, please let me know if you have a semester starting in February.

Franklin and Marshall's second semester begins in March. Gibbs was admitted for the second 1946 term. His record was poor from every point of view. He attributed his scholastic record to poor preparation at Pitman High, but that could not have been the case; the high school has always had an excellent record in preparing its pupils for higher education. They have been admitted to institutions with stiffer entrance requirements than those of Franklin and Marshall. Throughout his four years at college, Gibbs was placed on probation once and threatened with it a second and third time. The records at the school show a succession of failures. In his first term he failed General Inorganic Chemistry and the Mathematics of Finance, and escaped with D's in Elementary Spanish and English Composition. He made a

B in Economic Geography. The following semester his marks improved; he made three B's and a C, and was removed from probation. In the second semester of the sophomore year he failed Mathematics of Finance again and withdrew from Accounting because he was failing. He also failed in Religion. In the first half of his junior year he bounded back with an average of three C's and two D's, but during the next portion he failed Mathematics of Finance again and scored no higher than C in any subject. Mathematics of Finance is a required course for graduation with the degree of Bachelor of Science in Economics. He wearily prepared to take it a fourth time. At the start of his senior year he needed thirteen hours' credit to graduate. According to one college official, he could have achieved these credits if he had been industrious. He was not. Soon after the 1949–1950 term began it became obvious that he would inevitably flunk. His instructors could not understand why he did not study more, since he seemed inordinately conscious of the importance of getting ahead. When they asked about his lack of interest, he was unable to explain it. The college's file on Gibbs contains several notes from him asking to be released from courses. One reads:

> I am carrying a very heavy schedule and the work has been getting to hard to manage and I feel the dropping of this course will make the burden easier.

Gibbs was pledged to Sigma Pi, but for a time it appeared that his low grades might keep him from being initiated. At one point the president of the fraternity went to see the Dean of Men, A. G. Breidenstine, to ask about the status of Pledge Gibbs. Breidenstine agreed to offer no objection to his initiation if Gibbs would agree to tutor in Spanish. Once admitted to the fraternity, Gibbs became, or attempted to become, a popular and active brother. He was, one of the members has recalled, a dependable dance committeeman, and a fair bridge player, although his temper sometimes burst forth in the house games. In appearance, he was more careless than he had been in high school; he often dressed in old G.I. clothes and appeared tieless in classes. When it came time for a dance at the Sigma Pi house, however, his dress quickly underwent a change for the better. "He liked to think that he was one of the sharpest dressers in the school," one brother remembers.

If anything, Gibbs was more eager to be liked at F. & M. than he had been at Pitman. One friend believes this may have been due to the change in his appearance. He had put on weight in the Army, and was no longer as clean-faced as he had been in high school. Another friend believes that his feeling of inadequacy in college stemmed from his inability to star in athletics. He went out for the football team in 1947, and was carried that season by Coach Charles Soleau. He played in a limited number of games. During '48 spring training he reported to the new coaches, Woodrow and Boyd Sponaugle, and stayed with the squad until pre-season practice in the fall. At that time, Woodrow Sponaugle, himself a former F. & M. star, known for his tough, frank approach to his players, who admire him for it, said to Gibbs, "I think you like to hit but don't like to get hit." Gibbs is reported to have said, "That's kind of a relief to me, Coach." As usual, his emotionless façade was in place; he went off by himself and wept. In 1947 he had gone out for varsity basketball, but had failed to make the team. The only sport in which he excelled was golf. Max Hannum, assistant to President Distler, played with him several times at courses around

Lancaster. Hannum's age and position did not deter Gibbs from losing his temper when pressed too far. Hannum recalls:

"He was an ordinary golfer, not an exceptional one. He'd get sore if he missed a shot or if you talked him out of one. I remember one time we played in the early spring, and I hadn't been out since the year before. I made a joke, needled him a little bit, to talk him out of a shot. Well, he blasted me a few times. He accused me of not being a gentleman. He said, 'You're no gentleman—you're deliberately trying to get me upset and excited.' Next day he came into my office and apologized. He said, 'They tell me I made an ass of myself out on the course yesterday. I'm sorry. I don't remember doing it.'"

Lapses of memory of this kind were not uncommon in Hannum's experience with Gibbs. Hannum's son, Bob, entered the college and was rushed by the fraternities. Sigma Pi gave him the biggest play, but at the last minute he changed his mind and picked Phi Kappa Psi. The next day, Gibbs accosted Hannum and said, mildly, "We sure were sorry to lose Bob." And then, according to Hannum, he lost control. He said, among other things, "You've sure got a hell of a nerve interfering in fraternity matters—you should've let Bob make up his own mind." Hannum, protesting that he had done nothing to influence his son's choice, tried to get him to calm down, but was unsuccessful. Gibbs continued to rave. And as before, he looked up Hannum the next day and said, "Gee whizz, Max, I'm awfully sorry for the way they tell me I acted yesterday. Honestly, I don't remember a thing about it."

Soon after he was pledged to the fraternity, Gibbs brought Helen Woodward, a girl from Pitman, to one of the dances. Previously he had bragged to his brothers about the girl, and they had doubted that she could be as pretty as he claimed. To their astonishment, everything he said was true. Helen Woodward, at twenty-one, was a rare beauty. She had dark hair and eyes, delicate features and a calm, well-bred manner. In many ways she was the exact antithesis of her husband-to-be; she never raised her voice, her table manners left nothing to be desired, she was modest and self-effacing, and she appeared to have no strong, aggressive opinions on any subject. When Gibbs introduced her and made some such remark as, "See— isn't she as good-looking as I said she was?" she would smile as though embarrassed. The newspapers later said they had been high-school sweethearts, but they were wrong. Helen Gibbs had moved to Sewell, New Jersey, which is close to Pitman, the year after Gibbs graduated. She was the daughter of Mr. and Mrs. John Woodward, formerly of Haddonfield, New Jersey. Gibbs had not met her until after he returned from military service. Very little about Helen Gibbs can be set down here. She withdrew to her family's home in Sewell as soon as Gibbs was arrested, and her mother refused to allow her to speak either to reporters or to the defense attorney. The District Attorney, however, reported that she co-operated willingly whenever he called upon her. Her friends, both in Pitman and in Lancaster, formed a wall of protective silence around her which has never been penetrated. They refuse to discuss her except to say, "Helen's been through enough. She wants to forget."

Edward Gibbs and Helen Woodward were married February 1, 1947, in the First Presbyterian Church of Pitman, with the Reverend Glover Leitch reading the service. It was one of the biggest weddings ever held in the town. "Because of the prominence of the two families, everybody who was anybody was there," Reverend Leitch has said. Still, it is gossip around Pitman that the entire

Gibbs family felt that the wedding and the reception, which followed at Hotel Pitman, were not quite elaborate enough for so significant an occasion as the marriage of the male heir. The main reaction of Gibbs' old school friends was wonder. "We couldn't figure out how he'd snagged a girl as pretty as Helen," one has said. "It wasn't that he was *bad* looking, but he did have those buck teeth, and he was a spitter. People talking to him used to say, 'Why don't you pass out towels?' "

Gibbs proudly took his bride back to the campus. In court, he summed up his marriage as follows:

> A—We lived [first] at East Hall Dormitory, which is the dormitory used for married veterans at the college.
>
> Q—And did you continue to live there?
>
> A—Up until a year ago, I forget exactly when, but we moved to an apartment, 429 West Orange Street.
>
> Q—Then you moved back to the college?
>
> A—Then we moved back to the college after being in the apartment approximately a year.
>
> Q—Now, will you tell us briefly about how you and your wife got along?
>
> A—We got along all right. We were like any other young couple just married. We were struggling, we had our problems, both parents living in the same town, when we went home week-ends, caused a great deal of dissension between us because they both wanted us to be at their house. We didn't want to have a child, and yet we did. I mean we wanted a child but didn't feel we could afford it, and this caused us to

have a little bit of discussion, a little bit of disagreement on when we could start having a
child.

Q—Then are there any other events in
your married life you want to discuss . . . ?

A—No, sir, I don't think there is.

Dr. Strecker, after questioning Gibbs on his sex
relations with his wife, described the situation as follows:

"The sexual aspect of his marriage was not satisfactory. At first the young people did not desire a baby.
His wife refused to use a diaphragm and would not permit her husband to use any protective device. Apparently
Gibbs accepted this without much protest and withdrawal
was practiced. All psychologists agree that withdrawal
has a very harmful effect on the nervous system and the
personality. In the last part of their marriage, Gibbs did
not wish to have any sex relationship and had it only every
two or three months. The whole pattern of his sex life is
one of immaturity and inadequacy. These traits, as shown
in his sex life, are the reflection of his personality traits in
other relationships in life. I might have mentioned that
the marriage was pretty much dominated by his mother-
in-law who never liked him and who was against her
daughter marrying him."

(It ought to be added that in Helen Gibbs' view,
the marriage was dominated to a large degree by *her*
mother-in-law.)

Those who knew the young Gibbses in their first
months of marriage on the campus have reported that they
appeared deliriously happy. Helen seemed to have exer-
cised a considerable influence for the better on her husband. One friend says he began to pay more attention to

his studies, and seemed more serious and thoughtful. Yet he did not lose his sense of humor. "I liked Eddie," R— G—, a friend of the couple, has said. "He was a rah-rah college boy, all the time. He was very clothes conscious. Once he told me he was getting a corduroy jacket and white buck shoes, and he was so elated I had to laugh." Gibbs and Helen turned up at all the parties and dances and seemed to have a wonderful time together. Once they went to Philadelphia on a weekend with another couple. While the girls went shopping, Gibbs and the other young man and Gibbs' mother, who had come in from Pitman, went to a University of Pennsylvania football game. When the girls got back to the room, Helen found a note on her dresser. She blushed and said something like, "Oh, isn't he sweet!" She told her friend that he was always leaving attentive little notes around for her. To augment their small income, Helen went to work in an office at Armstrong Cork. Everyone there liked her; her employer later described her as an exceptionally good worker.

Gibbs' married life in his sophomore year apparently was without incident. It was while he was a junior that his friends first began to notice a change in his attitude toward Helen. "He became a table-hopper, kind of," one says. "They'd get to a party, and maybe have one dance, and then he'd be off talking to other guys—or mainly to their girls." A girl remembers, "He was always a great one for kissing you on the cheek, putting his arm around you, and making remarks that weren't dirty exactly, but weren't clean either. He made me a little uncomfortable." Gibbs sometimes made proposals to girls ("Let's go out to Long Park and neck") in a joking way, ostensibly; but some of them thought he was not joking at all. A neighbor who lived in the apartment building at 429 West Orange

Street recalls that one night he heard someone shouting in the Gibbs apartment. Another remembers that Helen looked tired and drawn much of the time she saw her during this period. None of those who were close to the couple believes that they quarreled often, but all feel that it would have been unlike Gibbs to control his temper. Nevertheless, they kept their dissension to themselves, and in public appeared as much in love as they had been the year before.

In the senior year the marriage began to disintegrate. Now there were debts. Gibbs had bought a car, a 1947 two-tone blue Chevrolet club coupé (he referred to it as "The Chevvy"). There were payments due on it. They borrowed $207.09 from Household Finance Company, agreeing to repay it in eleven monthly installments, the first to be $17.99 and each subsequent one to be $20.00. There were school and fraternity bills to be paid. Helen was still working at Armstrong, but her weekly paycheck amounted to less than $45.00. On top of the dismal financial pattern of their lives, or under it, was the continual argument over whether or not they should have a child. Helen desperately wanted one, her friends say. She felt, they believe, it might have done something to strengthen or bolster up their marriage. Gibbs was adamant. He was frantically eager to quit school; he saw no point in their continuing to live frugally in a situation neither liked when he might well have been out on a job, getting established for the future. Their living quarters were none too agreeable. East Hall was formerly a dormitory of Franklin and Marshall Academy, a preparatory school which went out of existence just prior to World War II. It is more than fifty years old; its floors creak and its walls have been patched and re-patched. Gibbs and his wife lived in Room

421, on the second floor, the room next to the southeast corner of the building. It was a high-ceilinged room measuring about twelve feet square. The walls were painted a peach color, the woodwork was off-white. It was furnished with college-issued pieces: two plain dressers, a foldout bed, and three straight chairs. The rent was $70 per month. The couple augmented the room's equipment with some possessions of their own, mainly wedding presents: an electric iron, an electric fan, an electric hair dryer, a picture of Helen Gibbs on one dresser, a Guest Book, a table lamp, a floor lamp, a card table, a straight-legged table, a silver cigarette lighter, a hamper for soiled clothes, and a candy jar in which they were saving pennies. It was an inconvenient, uncomfortable dwelling at best, and its shoddiness must have made Gibbs feel somewhat ashamed of his inability to do better for his wife. Still, she did not complain. She was glad to be with him, and she would have lived in worse circumstances if necessary. "Helen was never as conscious of position and material things as Eddie was," one girl friend of hers has said.

It is not known, and possibly never will be, if Helen Gibbs was aware that she was married to a potentially violent personality, but there is one conclusive bit of evidence proving that she began to worry about him toward the middle of his junior year. The Veterans' Administration maintained a Guidance Center on the Franklin and Marshall Campus. At the urging of his wife and a friend, Gibbs went there to take some tests. The psychologist who administered them does not remember which tests they were. He later made a resumé of his findings and turned it over to Gibbs' defense attorney. It says, in part:

"Claimant is a junior . . . who has had a rather unimpressive record . . . in the Pitman, New Jersey, High School he obviously worked below his ability level . . . All of his . . . grades were in the low 70's with the exception of social studies where he was close to 80. In the service he began cadet training but states that he was "washed out" due to hayfever. He then served 14 months as control tower operator. In recent summers he has been employed as a laboratory technician and a crane operator. At F & M his scholastic attainment has paralleled his high school record. . . . It is interesting to note that his highest grades average has always been earned in the semester following a poor record. This, plus the personality picture and intelligence level, suggests that he is typically extroverted and not the serious student type. Testing indicates that he could average C− in college, that his interests are in the persuasive and social service fields, that he has average mathematical and clerical aptitude for business and his total personal picture is very similar to that of salesman. Typically, claimant failed to complete advisement because of the "pressure of other activities." He is now employed part-time as a sales representative of a New Jersey trucking concern (while completing college). He is probably devoting a great deal more time to this than to academic work. He will probably be very successful in the sales field. Since claimant failed to return to center, no objective was selected, and case was placed in SUSPENDED STATUS.

The psychologist has recalled that he wanted to give Gibbs a Rorschach test; he declares that there was enough information available in Gibbs' scores in the other tests to indicate that if he was not specifically sick, he was greatly disturbed and in need of some help. Gibbs, who sensed enough of this to refuse to believe it, declared that his job with the trucking company didn't give him enough time. "I wouldn't have time to do this Guidance work," he said reasonably. By then he had decided to follow his father's bent and become a traffic manager. The trucking job was meant to be preparation for his future. He had pleaded with his parents several more times to allow him to leave school, but they had refused to alter their attitude. Helen, too, thought he should finish. Gibbs's unrest at Franklin and Marshall was delineated in a Student Appraisal made by several of his instructors and signed by Horace R. Barnes. It was executed December 8, 1949, and said:

> *Judgment*—others cannot depend upon his decisions.
> *Initiative*—independent worker; gives good suggestions; moderately aggressive.
> *Industry*—takes things easy; does enough to get by.
> *Co-operation*—usually willing to co-operate.
> *Leadership*—can lead in small groups.
> *Appearance*—usually presentable.
> *Accomplishment in relation to capacity*—below average.
> *Emotional stability*—good.
> *Comments*—"Mr. Gibbs does not seem to care about anything."

"Convincing and persuasive speaker, but short on real work. I should say he is just getting by."

Edward and Helen Gibbs went home to Pitman for the 1949 Christmas Holidays. There was the usual argument about where they would stay; they compromised by staying part of the time at both parents' houses. This argument was more bitter than others, for matters were now approaching a climax. During that vacation, Gibbs went through another depressing emotional experience with his family. Describing it in court, he said,

Q—Now, then, Ed, how were you doing in your classes in your Senior Year, 1949–1950?

A—Not good at all, sir. I was flunking a great deal.

Q—What, particularly, were you having trouble with?

A—Psychology and Spanish.

Q—Did you realize this at Christmastime, this past Christmas?

A—Yes, sir.

Q—And what happened?

A—I went home on Christmas vacation and the subject of graduation came up between my mother and I, and I told her that there was a possibility that I wouldn't graduate, and she got very excited about it, she started to cry and say about not seeing me in a cap and gown and everything, and I immediately laughed it off, covered up, said I was going to graduate, not to worry about it, I was just kidding her.

Q—Did you realize you weren't going to graduate?

A—Yes, sir, I fully realized I wasn't going to graduate.

Q—How did it affect you when your mother was upset?

A—It hit me very deep because I always tried to make good for my parents and family and I knew they placed a lot of emphasis on my graduating from college.

Gibbs returned to the campus on January 3, 1950. During the following week he was in a terrible emotional state. The worries, fears, guilts and doubts inside him could be contained no longer. They had to be released; he had to do something—to release them, to prove to himself he was a man, and to prove it to the world. He could not have been consciously aware of his need; he could never have articulated it in detail. If it had been suggested to him, he probably would have scoffed. Intimations of inner violence are intolerable to one so bent upon being socially acceptable. They exist only in others; in less respectable people, not in fraternity brothers or athletes or campus politicians. Yet the powerfully assertive impulses were there, and the conscious of Edward Gibbs shut itself off, for a time, and obeyed its lower, darker brother. On Tuesday, January 10, 1950, he met Marian Louise Baker, took her for a ride, and killed her. How he committed this crime will be described presently.

So strong in Gibbs were the twin desires for conformity and approval that he was unable to say, later, exactly why he killed the girl. He must have been aware, if only vaguely, of the nature of the resentment stirring inside him. It could not have failed to show itself to him in dreams; but perhaps he was unable to interpret them, or unwilling. In prison, he said once to Dr. Keyes, "I was under great pressure, deep inside me." Yet he was fanatically anxious to suppress it, perhaps without knowing that he was; or he had to ignore it, to pretend that it did not exist, in order to permit himself the stability he needed to continue to function through the days. He said, stubbornly repeating it, "I did it on an impulse." He would not, perhaps could not, say more. The word "impulse" evidently seemed to him to be explanation and justification enough. In a way, he used it as self-protection; he hid behind it against the evils moiling inside him—the evils which exist in us all, to some degree, but which, in Edward Gibbs' view, could not possibly have existed in Edward Gibbs. The closest he ever came to self-understanding, or to admitting that he had become his other nature's tool, was when he said that he might not have killed Marian Baker if he could have done something else, such as hurl a rock through a window. He indicated that this act might have soothed him, at least for the moment. By so saying he was again demonstrating his total incapacity, or total reluctance, to understand himself. Breaking a window would not have satisfied him, for in battering Marian Baker's head to an almost unrecognizable mass he was not merely killing her. All his life, women had loomed over him as vicious symbols of authority, tantalizing, shadowy mistresses who controlled him and yet who taunted him by remaining ever out of grasp. While they used him as they wished, they whispered that he could dominate them—but he could not. They were too tricky, too elusive, too ultimately unattainable. Every mundane problem comfronting him on the afternoon of January tenth was in some way connected with a woman. He could not bear it. The hostility, festering per-

94

haps from the time he had been trained to the toilet, screamed for release. He did not simply kill Marian Baker. He killed his mother, teachers in school who had twisted him into learning, nurses in the Army hospital, whores in Italy, laughing and witless Pitman girls, his wife, his wife's friends, his friends' wives and girls, girls he saw on Lancaster and Pitman streets, girls he observed while at work in his various part-time jobs, every girl and every woman he had hated and simultaneously wanted. He murdered them all. He did not know it, and few others did. He said "impulse," and society, while convinced he was lying, had to take him at his word—conceivably for the same self-protective, self-deceptive reasons that prompted him to say it.

Those who later looked for some driven, Dostoievskian exhibitions from Gibbs in the days immediately following his crime were astonished to learn that he comported himself in a fairly "normal" manner. He at first thought of going to the police and confessing, and immediately decided against it. He later said to Dr. Keyes,

"I felt sick all over the body. The next few days were awful. I wanted to be alone, and was afraid to be alone. Every car, every person, every stranger brought fear to me. . . . I think I had a headache all this time."

Something in Gibbs made it necessary for him to let himself open to suspicion. He approached two undertakers' sons on the campus and asked each how long it would ordinarily take a body to decompose. About the time that the police were pulling Marian Baker's mangled body out of the cavity beneath the Harnish cottage, Gibbs was in the Pitman Police Headquarters, which is located on Broadway in the same building that houses the public library, asking questions of Frank Y. Hinkle, department clerk. Gibbs asked Hinkle if it was possible to obtain fingerprints from a dead person's body. Hinkle said it was. Gibbs then asked how long it could be done after a person had died. Hinkle said he didn't know. That same day, Gibbs visited S. Ephraim Burkett, a Pitman undertaker. A memorandum in the Lancaster District Attorney's files describes this visit as follows:

[GIBBS] TOLD HIM THAT HE HAD SEVERAL QUESTIONS THAT HE LIKED TO ASKED RELATIVE TO THE DECOMPOSITION OF THE HUMAN BODY AS HE WOULD BE GETTING SOME QUESTIONS ALONG THIS LINE IN HIS EXAMINATION ON THE SUBJECT OF CRIMINOLOGY. HE THEN ASKED MR. BURKETT HOW LONG IT WOULD TAKE A HUMAN BODY TO DECOMPOSE, LAYING ON THE SURFACE OF THE GROUND, INTERRED IN THE EARTH, WRAPPED IN A BLANKET, AND FINALLY HOW LONG IF THE BODY WAS PLACED IN A COFFIN AND THE REGULAR PROCEDURE FOLLOWED. GIBBS THEN ASKED IF IT WAS POSSIBLE TO OBTAIN FINGERPRINTS FROM A BODY OF A DEAD PERSON. HE STATED, FOR EXAMPLE, IF I HAD CHOKED SOMEONE, COULD MY FINGERPRINTS BE TAKEN FROM THE NECK OF THE DEAD PERSON.

Both the police and Burkett thought nothing of these questions at the time. The police said, "Because of his spotless reputation and his family's prominence, we did not connect him with the slaying." Oddly enough, however, he was questioned about it. An old friend from Gibbs' days as a basketball star, met him in Jerry Cherubino's pool room on Saturday afternoon. He asked Gibbs, purely as a joke, what he knew about the murder. Gibbs made some half-joking reply; no one recalls what it was. He is reported to have said, confidently, a few hours later, "They'll never get the guy who did that." Another acquaintance happened to see Gibbs on the street that day. He knew that Gibbs had never been much of a drinker, but he thought to himself: that boy looks as though he's got an awful hangover. Other Pitman people who saw him recall nothing unusual about his appearance.

The events subsequent to his crime and prior to his confession became a melange in Gibbs' mind, perhaps because his subconscious wished to protect itself, perhaps because his conscious refused to acknowledge what he had done. He returned to Franklin and Marshall from Pitman on Sunday night. Sometime during the next few days he attempted to establish an alibi with his friend, John K. George, who had gone downtown with him on the afternoon that he had met Marian Baker. In testimony, George described this as follows:

> Q—Did you have a conversation with him, or did he have one with you concerning the time you were down at the movies?
>
> A—Well, he reminded me or said something to me to the effect we were together until 2:30.
>
> Q—You were reminded that you were together until 2:30 the previous Tuesday?
>
> *
>
> A—I believe at the time we were discussing that we were downtown that afternoon if we should be questioned.
>
> Q—This was on the general subject of the Marian Baker case, is that right?

A—Yes.

Q—This was—was this after the body had been found?

A—I'm not sure of that. I don't really recall.

Q—But you were talking about the Marian Baker case?

A—Yes, we discussed it.

Q—And the general conversation was, if you were questioned he suggested you had been together until 2:30 on that Tuesday?

A—Yes.

Helen Gibbs, like all wives on the campus, discussed the murder with her husband. He did not say much about it. She later confided to a friend that she was afraid to go out on the campus at night unless she was with Eddie. Most of the wives shared her fear; they were sure that the murderer might strike again. This was a general reaction in Lancaster soon after Marian Baker's body was discovered. Several parents refused to allow their daughters to go on dates with F. & M. boys.

Gibbs was going through incredible torment. Each time he heard the case discussed or read something about it in the paper, he felt a wild urge to go and tell someone the truth. Several times he was on the verge of confiding in Helen. On Wednesday morning, he arose with his resolve *not* to tell reinforced; he was certain that if they suspected him, they would have picked him up already. From what he had read and from the gossip going about the campus, he was almost positive that the investigation was going badly for the police. Coincidentally, that was the very day the investigators finally got around to thinking about acting on the tip that Dean Breidenstine had held out to them Monday morning, the tip concerning the student who had inquired from another the length of time it ordinarily takes a body to decompose. At two P.M. Detective Frank Matt and Corporal James Kane walked into the Dean's office and asked him to repeat his theory. He outlined it for them patiently. Matt asked if he could call Gibbs in. The Dean asked his secretary to send out a message summoning Gibbs. She called and left word at East Hall, at the library, and at the Sigma Pi house, but Gibbs was at none of those places.

The officers waited approximately one hour and left for another appointment with Max Hannum. Before going, they asked the Dean to please keep Gibbs from knowing that they were looking for him.

Gibbs arrived at the Dean's office shortly after the policemen left. He said he had had a message at the fraternity house, and that someone had stopped him on the way over and told him he was wanted. "He was rushing in quite a sweat," the Dean recalls. "He was all in a dither." The Dean had to think fast, remembering the officer's warning. An incident which he had heard some time before came to his mind.

His voice calm, he said, "Ed, what was that blowup in Spanish class about?" (Sometime previously, Gibbs had been in a violent argument with his Spanish professor.)

"It wasn't anything serious," Gibbs said.

"You're too adult to act in that manner," said the Dean sternly. He went on lecturing for a moment, and ended with the admonition, "You've got to learn to control yourself, Ed."

Gibbs had stood impatiently throughout the dean's speech. When the latter finished, he said, "Is that all, sir?"

Breidenstine nodded. Gibbs left the office as hastily as he had entered it. The secretary later reported to the

Dean that he left muttering to himself; she did not remember exactly what it was, but it was something to this effect: "Imagine the Dean calling *me* in and calling me down for a little thing like that!"

He had fallen for the Dean's story, and it gave him a temporary sense of security; before going to the office, he had been certain that the police wanted him. Now he could breathe for a while. The feeling quickly vanished when he saw two officers with Tom Floyd, the athletic trainer. After killing Marian Baker, he had borrowed a shovel from the athletic equipment room to attempt to dig her grave. He was certain that Floyd was telling the officers about the shovel. Nearly in a panic, he half ran across the campus to East Hall, scrambled up the stairs, and went into his room. Helen, of course, was at work. He did not turn on a light. He sat there, breathing heavily through his mouth. It is not known how long he sat there. Eventually he rose and went out into the hall. He walked to the stairwell and looked out over the campus through a window.

What he saw must have made him shake with terror.

Two officers were looking over his parked car, examining it minutely. It was then that he knew he could not stand the waiting any more. He flung himself down the stairs three at a time, ran through the door, across the campus to College Avenue, up College to West James Street, and down to the Sigma Pi house. There he sought out his friend John George, who later testified as to what he said. Here is the dialogue as George was questioned in court:

Q—Now, John, will you tell me what conversation you had with this defendant on

100

January 18, 1950, which, I believe, was a Wednesday?

A—Well, I went to the Fraternity house about 3:00 o'clock in the afternoon. I was playing bridge in the game room of the Fraternity House. Ed came in, I am not sure what time it was, it must have been around 4:30 or quarter of 5:00.

Q—Proceed.

A—And he called me outside of the Fraternity House, came to the door of the game room and asked if he could talk to me. I went outside and he handed me the keys to his car and asked me to pick up his wife after work at 5:00 o'clock.

*

Q—What else did he say?

A—Well, he had done that before and I didn't think anything of it. I asked him where he was going. At the time there had been a note on the bulletin board or mirror in the Fraternity House to report to Dean Breidenstine's office.

Q—For whom?

A—Eddie. I asked if it was about that. He said, "This is about Spanish," referring to the note about Dean Breidenstine. I asked where he was going and he sort of blurted out he was going over to discuss to Dean Breidenstine, to confess he had killed Marian Baker.

Q—He said that in your presence?

A—Yes, in my presence.

101

Q—Did anybody else besides you hear the conversation?

A—No, there wasn't.

Q—Then what happened?

A—Well, I didn't believe him the first time, but the second time he repeated it I believed him, because he said it in such a way I just believed him.

Q—. . . He is a close friend of yours; is that correct?

A—That is correct.

Q—And he said to you—what were his words, if you can recall them?

A—That he was going over to confess; that he was going over to Dean Breidenstine's office to confess he had killed Marian Baker.

Q—He repeated it twice?

A—I am not sure whether he repeated the same words twice, but he repeated it.

Q—And the second time you believed him?

A—I believed him.

Q—Did you go out later and pick up his wife?

A—I went out from there and picked up his wife.

Gibbs left the startled George, but instead of going to the Dean's office, for some reason he headed straight for the office of Dr. Theodore A. Distler, the President.

Max Hannum, Gibbs' sometime golfing companion, was then in Dr. Distler's office. He had gone there to consult with the President about a speech the latter was to make. The President's office is separated from his secretary's anteroom by two old-fashioned sliding doors. Dr. Distler is an accessible, convivial soul; he customarily keeps these doors open. By that time the campus was overrun with reporters, not only from the Lancaster papers, but also from those in Philadelphia, Reading, Baltimore, York, Harrisburg and other near-by cities and towns. Two Baltimore reporters were lounging in the anteroom, hoping for a break of some sort.

Gibbs came in hurriedly, his face flushed, and said to Myrtle Doner, the secretary, "I want to see those men in there" he gestured toward Hannum and the President— "they're my friends."

"I'm sorry," said Myrtle Doner, "but they're busy right now. They're in conference."

The reporters paid no particular attention to the excited young man. They were standing by looking bored in the immemorial manner of the incurious American journalist.

"I'm going in anyway," Gibbs said, in a frenzied voice. Before the secretary could stop him, he started for the office.

The two men inside, recalling the Monday-morning conference, had exchanged significant glances. They nevertheless decided to pretend ignorance. Hannum waved as Gibbs started toward him. "Hi, Ed," he said cheerily.

"Hello, Edward," said Dr. Distler.

Gibbs said, "I—understand you have been looking for me."

"Why, no," said Hannum, "not particularly."

"Yes, you have been looking for me."

"Sit down, Edward," said Dr. Distler, kindly.

"I am Edward Gibbs," said Gibbs, hysterically.

"Yes, Ed, we know you," said Hannum.

"No," said Gibbs, "you don't know me. You just

think you know me." He drew a faltering breath. "I did it. I am the man you are looking for."

"Sit down, Ed," said Hannum.

"You did what, Edward?" asked Dr. Distler.

"I killed Marian Baker," said Gibbs.

Hannum only then caught sight of the reporters. He gave the President a significant look, raised his voice and said, "No, sir, I don't think that's the way you spell it."

"Spell what?" asked Dr. Distler, in bewilderment.

"*Laissez faire,*" said Hannum, still speaking in a moderate shout.

Gibbs, as bewildered as the President had been, sank into a chair and sat there with his hands clenched between his knees. He was wearing an Army leather jacket, a shirt with no tie, and Army denim pants.

Hannum put his head out the door. "Myrtle," he said, "will you please look up in the dictionary how to spell *laissez faire?*"

"What are you talking about?" she asked.

"*Laissez faire,*" said Hannum. "A French word."

"*Laissez faire,*" called Dr. Distler, who had caught on.

The secretary looked up the word and reported the proper spelling. By then the reporters, divining that the conference inside would take some time, had gone out.

Dr. Distler said to Gibbs, "You'd better be awfully certain about this, Edward. I think you're a little hysterical."

"I did it," Gibbs repeated. "I have no idea why I did it."

"Are you *absolutely* sure?" Hannum said.

"I did it," said Gibbs.

"You have—ah—certain legal rights," said Dr. Distler, in the same kindly tone.

Gibbs began to cry. "I am absolutely sure. If you come with me I can show you things that will prove it to you. Oh, I've disgraced my wife, my family and my college!" He looked up at Hannum tearfully. "I don't want to die, Max. I don't have to die, do I?"

Dr. Distler looked at Hannum bleakly. "Where are they now, Max?"

"In my office," said Hannum. He picked up the telephone and dialed his secretary. "Are Matt and Kane still there? Tell them to wait for me; I'll be right over." He touched Gibbs on the shoulder. "Come, Ed."

Gibbs stood up like a man under hypnosis. Hannum escorted him down the hall to the rear entrance of the building. By then Gibbs had dried his tears.

"Where are we going?"

"I'm going to take you to my office," said Hannum, "and introduce you to some gentlemen there."

At the door, Gibbs said, "Aren't you going to take hold of me?"

"Why, no," said Hannum. "I'm no officer."

The two golfing friends walked across the campus, nodding to people they knew. At Hannum's office, he told his two secretaries to leave. The officers looked up expectantly.

"Gentlemen," said Hannum, "This is Ed Gibbs, and he has something to tell you."

"I'm the guy who killed Marian Baker," said Gibbs, brokenly.

The policemen began questioning him. Hannum remained in the background, ready to be of assistance. When the time came for the officers to take Gibbs away, he turned to Hannum. There was an expression on his face that somehow communicated gratitude for the older man's kindness.

Gibbs said, "You know those woods of mine you liked when we were playing golf?"

"Yes, Ed, I remember them."

"You can have them. I guess I won't be needing them any more."

Hannum did not know what to answer.

Gibbs took off his Sigma Pi ring. "Will you please see that Helen gets this?"

Hannum took the ring. The policemen took the murderer away.

6

The Trial

Lancaster city's downtown business district is a square, bounded on the north by Chestnut Street and on the south by Vine, on the east by Duke and on the west by Prince. Queen Street, the main drag, runs north and south through the center of this square. It is crossed in the middle of Penn Square, the center of town, by the east-and-west King, another artery, and it is crossed one block north of King by Orange, yet another. Dead center in Penn Square is a monument to the Lancaster countians who died in the Civil War. It was erected in 1874. Traffic-minded civic groups sometimes propose moving the monument to Buchanan Park or some other spot where it will be less of an impediment; other groups set up a cry of protest, and the monument continues to sit inexorably while traffic loops around it. The stores, shops and offices in downtown Lancaster are those of any city of comparable size. Some are home-owned, some are parts of chains, some are locally owned with national affiliations.

The block of Duke Street that runs between Orange

and King is technically in the commercial section, since it is part of the eastern boundary, but is older, less busy, and more pleasant to look at than the other central streets. The approximately 110 members of the Lancaster County Bar have their offices on both sides, and the block is popularly called Lawyers' Row despite the intrusion of the gas company offices, the stock exchange, a bowling alley, and a scattering of realtors, building-and-loan associations and travel bureaus. Like that of most American cities, the face of Lancaster has been undergoing a slow chrome-and-plastic surgical operation for the past twenty-five years, but the visage of this old street has remained much as it was a half-century ago. Some of the buildings are nearly as old as the city itself. The one at the northeast corner of Grant Street, the alley behind the courthouse which intersects Duke, was erected nearly two centuries ago. A brass tablet bolted to its front by the Lancaster County Historical Society says that Henry Muhlenberg, a leader among the pioneer botanists of America, lived there from 1780 until he died in 1815. The other buildings are not as old, but they are, nevertheless, venerable. They are somewhat like the older judges and interpreters and practitioners of the law who work along their damp corridors; they have settled comfortably into their chosen places on the street, and sit like two rows of sages facing each other. Their floors tilt a bit as though cramped by neuralgia, but their seams and cracks are those of seasoned dignity, not decrepitude. Tradition is strong among older families in Lancaster, and several sons have followed fathers and grandfathers down Duke Street, past the two old maples on the west side, into the dark offices of the old structures. Among these is the attorney who was chosen to defend Edward Lester Gibbs. His name is W. Hensel Brown. His father, John Hay Brown, was a

108

justice of the Supreme Court of Pennsylvania from 1900 to 1915, and Chief Justice from then until 1921. Judge Brown had begun practicing in Lancaster in 1871; in the early 1890's, he had formed a partnership with William Uhler Hensel, for whom he named his younger son. Judge Brown's older son, J. Hay Brown, Jr., is also an attorney practicing on Lawyers' Row. Both sons graduated from college with AB degrees and promptly entered their father's office to read the law in preparation for the state board examinations.

W. Hensel, called Hense by his friends (he dropped the William because there were a number of William Browns in Lancaster), was born in 1902. He went to Franklin and Marshall Academy in Lancaster and then to college at Mount St. Mary's, in Emmitsburg, Maryland, where he played end on the football team with such distinction that he was named to an All-Maryland eleven in 1921. He went into his father's office in 1922 and passed his examinations in 1925. In 1932 he formed a partnership with the late federal judge Guy K. Bard. In 1938 the partnership was dissolved after Bard was appointed to the federal bench. Brown then practiced alone until 1948, at which time he formed a partnership with Bernard M. Zimmerman, a man five years his junior.

Brown does not look fifty. His eyes are dark and sharply inquiring. He has an acquiline nose and a face which seems to be composed of vertical lines. He is in excellent condition, stands five feet, eleven inches, and carries himself like an officer. He has a deep, carrying, actor's voice, but without an actor's self-consciousness. It has served him well in representing men and women accused of everything from petty thievery to murder, but the appearance, the voice and his sense of drama are among his minor assets. Brown has an intimate knowledge of criminal code and a splendid memory for minutiae, and although he is active in upper-register social activities in Lancaster, he is one of those rare Lancastrians who does find time to read. He is a student of Lincoln. His manner is affable, he has a well-defined sense of humor, and he gets along with his peers and his clients. His temper is sometimes shorter than he could desire; he has been known to pound tables to emphasize points. Ever since he and Zimmerman formed their partnership they have been successful.

Brown has been married since 1929 to the former Helen Gilson, and they have three sons and a daughter. The eldest son was born in 1930. The family lives in a large white house in Glen Moore Circle, one of the better residential sections located just outside the Lancaster city limits. They belong to the Lancaster County Club, and Hense is a member of the Hamilton Club, an exclusive men's organization located in the same block as Lawyers' Row. He also belongs to the Union League Club of Philadelphia. He was a delegate to the Republican National Convention which nominated Dwight D. Eisenhower.

During the past ten years, Brown has been devoting less and less time to criminal cases. He has by no means given them up entirely, and he has no intention of so doing, but his civil practice—corporation law and the handling of trusts and estates—is equally remunerative and, at the same time, less demanding, physically and emotionally. His interest has shifted partly because of the continual urging of his wife and of his secretary, Lillian Hess Kurtz, who has been with him since 1929. Both women have always maintained that the defense of criminal actions takes too much out of him. Some lawyers have trained themselves to a professional detachment which enables them to view their clients purely as vehicles of commerce.

110

Brown has this characteristic, too, up to the point where a case becomes challenging; then, before he knows what is happening, he finds himself entangled in the extra-legal, human aspects. Whenever this occurs he castigates himself with a lecture on the desirability of keeping aloof and makes a silent vow that he will never again become involved, but he recognizes that he is incurable and accepts it with philosophical resignation.

When Edward Gibbs confessed to the murder of Marian Louise Baker, the news leaked immediately. It went up and down Lawyers' Row as though each secretary were equipped with telegraphic apparatus, and it went out from there. The news leaked in the late afternoon, too late to be printed in the *New Era;* but thanks to Lancastrians' habit of keeping nothing to themselves, half the town knew it before the *Intelligencer Journal* came out at two the following morning.

Lillian Hess Kurtz at the time was ill in St. Joseph's Hospital, but the news was quickly relayed to her by one of her friends among the Lawyers' Row secretarial brigade. She surmised that Brown would be approached to take the case, and she began to hope that he would refuse. When Brown called to inquire after her health, she made some guarded reference to it. He replied blandly that he had heard nothing. That evening, when he arrived home, his wife also referred to it. Neither woman put her feelings into specific sentences, thereby sparing Brown the necessity of assuring them of his disinclination to become a part of the business. Brown, when he had heard of the confession, had automatically, perhaps with a conscious effort, put the idea of his own involvement out of his mind. He did not mention it to his wife at dinner. Afterward they went into their sunporch, which they have converted into a television room, and watched the programs on WGAL-TV until about ten thirty, when they retired. Around eleven, as Brown was dozing off, the telephone rang.

The caller was Dr. James Z. Appel, a prominent Lancaster physician who is connected with Franklin and Marshall College. He was telephoning from the Lancaster County Jail. He did not explain what he was doing there; he did not have to.

He said, half apologetically, yet with a note of urgency, "Hense, I don't want to get you into something you don't want to get into . . . but would you come out here and give some advice to this boy's family?"

Brown said, "Jim, there wouldn't be anything I could do for them tonight, even if I got up and came out. Tell them to try to get some rest. I'll see them in the morning." He went back to bed, but he did not go to sleep for a while.

Later, Brown said to a friend, "What could I do?" There were several things he could have done. He could have refused to take the case. He could suddenly have found several other civil matters with which to occupy his time. He could have pleaded a full schedule of criminal actions. He said only, "I'll see them in the morning."

Around two P.M. the next day he received Roy C. Gibbs and an attorney from Camden who had come up with him. Gibbs explained that he was a Shriner and about to be installed as an officer. It evidently was one of the most important things that had happened in his life. He wondered if, under the circumstances, he should . . . well, he wondered what he *should* do. Brown said he did not know how to advise him on this issue. Brown later agreed to accept the defense of Edward Gibbs on one condition. He said, "You must not expect me to do more

112

than try to save your nephew's life. From what I've read and heard, it looks like first degree murder to me."

In retelling the events of that crucial day in his life, Brown has said, "I remember I was very emphatic. I told them over and over that it looked like first degree murder. They said they understood that. 'Yes,' they kept saying, 'I understand.' I cannot tell too much of this because it would be violating confidence. I told them over and over that it looked that way to me. I told them I didn't want them to get any false hopes, and on the basis of that understanding I agreed to take the case." Brown was still the craftsman agreeing to the difficult, but not impossible, custom job. If he could have held to this role and preserved his lawyer's objectivity, he would have been spared much.

His first meeting with J. Lester and Florence Gibbs, that same week, did nothing to alter his attitude. Those two stricken, dumbfounded people bore up well, considering. They bore up because they were bolstered by a blind and conditioned inner force. They were like residents of a place destroyed by some unforeseen catastrophe; they knew what had happened, they were trying to grasp the fact that it had, and yet, because they were so totally unconditioned for anything resembling it, because it was unimaginably far from their personal frame of reference, they still were unable to bring themselves to accept it. A forfeit we pay for the many shields we have erected and devised to ease and protect our lives is our inability, in moments of shock, to realize that those people who weep over corpses in the *Daily Mirror* are not created by its cynical deskmen—that they are as real as we, and that similar things can happen to us with similar suddenness. The crime of Edward Gibbs was never a reality to his parents. Their grief was boundless, but it was, fortunately for their sanity, uncomprehending. Eddie could not have done such a thing, because Eddie would not have done such a thing; their world was constructed on Eddie; Eddie had done it, people said, *but he had not done it;* not Eddie. Yet there it was, and there was the necessity of seeking help. At such times we turn frantically to any new ally without a preliminary investigation such as we might make as a matter of routine. The Gibbs parents had been told that Brown might aid them; they walked into his office and gave themselves over to him. They groped into their son's past, they examined his life as they knew it; they poured out every pertinence that occurred to them, holding back only those which they must have felt could not have been germane—those minor details which might in any way have mitigated Brown's view of them as people of eminently respectable worth. Their relatives, also, and some of their friends, tried to be equally helpful, and tried to re-emphasize the Gibbs' position. Brown's file on the Edward Gibbs case is six inches thick.

The parents told Brown of the time their boy had fallen off the auto running board, and the time when he had been knocked out and robbed. They said he had acted "in an unusual manner" over the Christmas vacation; that he hadn't been himself." They were certain he was worried about his grades at school. Then they mentioned an incident that had occurred one weekend during the previous November (eventually Brown ascertained that the exact date was November 6, 1949), when Dr. French J. Friedlin, a Pitman physician, and his wife were dinner guests at the Gibbs home. In testimony, the doctor said:

> . . . I had dinner with the parents of the defendant at which he and his wife were also

present. During the course of dinner conversation of socialized medicine was brought up and Edward took a very decided view on that point and said, well, whether we liked it or not, it would have to come to government control of all things, business and otherwise, and the more he talked the faster he seemed to talk and the louder he got, and he finally terminated banging the table so hard that it moved a lot of the dishes and you could hardly understand what he was talking about. And my wife, who was sitting next to him, I could see was fidgeting just a little, and the latter part of his conversation you could hardly understand at all. . . . Well, he was highly nervous and emotionally upset, it seemed. The topic didn't seem to warrant the degree of excitement that he seemed to get . . .

During his initial meeting with the family, and several times thereafter, Brown reiterated that he could do no more than attempt to save the boy's life. They said they were aware of this, but it seemed to Brown then, and later, that they were in the grip of futile optimism, possibly a desperate device of self-protection. As they could not quite understand what their only child had done, so they could not allow themselves to believe that he would never be free again. At one time J. Lester Gibbs expressed the hope that if the boy were given a life sentence, he might well expect a parole within twenty years. This has often occurred in Pennsylvania, and it has occurred frequently in the cases of murderers sentenced from Lancaster County. To the Gibbs parents it was their one hope; they were sure it would happen to Eddie. Brown therefore was tempted to have Gibbs plead guilty and throw himself on the mercy of the court. He knew that neither judge in the Lancaster County court of Quarter Sessions had ever sentenced a man to death; he was willing to risk the chance that neither would mete out the ultimate penalty in this case. The parents would not permit him to plead their boy guilty. Later, Brown reproached himself for not having made a stronger argument to the parents. It was the first of many doubts he was to have in reconsidering his role in the affair, and the first step of the personal embattlement which was to bring him more torment and despair than he had ever experienced.

The mother and father quieted somewhat during that first conference. Mrs. Gibbs said that she had spoken with Eddie's wife. Helen had promised that she would stand by her husband. This was a good sign, Brown felt; the spectacle of the wife in the courtroom might have a marked effect upon the jury. He felt, too, that from all indications the boy was a mental case, and that he might hope for a charge of murder in the second degree.

Brown first met Edward Gibbs in the attorney's room at the Lancaster County Prison, a poorly illuminated, arch-ceilinged room with sickly green paint on the walls. From the outside, the prison's heavy stone walls and turrets make it resemble a feudal castle. The main entrance is a heavy lattice of thick iron bands. Inside, the building is damp and gloomy and has an ancient, musty odor. When Gibbs had been brought to the jail, Warden Walter N. Foust had put him in a cell just to the left of the entrance to the main block, one of several reserved for people awaiting trial. He had not issued the prisoner a uniform, since he was not officially an inmate. Gibbs had sat on the wooden bunk of the cold, high-walled, whitewashed cubbyhole, lighted only by a barred slit near the ceiling, shivering in the same jacket, pants and shirt he had been

116

wearing when he confessed. When they brought him in to meet Brown, his face was at first composed; but when he saw that his Uncle Roy was there, he broke into tears.

"Eddie," said Roy C. Gibbs gently, "you realize what you have done, don't you?"

"Yes, yes," Gibbs said, ". . . I could get the chair."

Brown talked quietly, trying to calm and reassure him, but Gibbs was held by uncontrollable, incoherent remorse for the better part of the interview. Brown cautioned him to say nothing to anyone regarding his situation and promised to return and see him again the next day. It was hardly a satisfactory session from the lawyer's point of view. Neither were any of the others, from then on until the day of the trial. Brown saw Gibbs every other day until February fourth, when he and his wife went to Palm Beach for a three-week vacation. That holiday haunted him for months after the trial, for he was certain that if he had not gone off, he might have been able to get closer to Gibbs. It is hard to see how he might have accomplished that, for Gibbs, as though he had been bidden, clung stubbornly to the same story he had told in his confession. He said only that he had killed Marian Baker "on impulse." He would say no more. Brown today sometimes says that he does not know how he could have prepared a better defense, and he is neither excusing his eventual failure nor permitting himself an unaccustomed excursion into pride. It is fact, and must be regarded as such on the basis of his severe, exhaustive interrogation of Gibbs in those numerous conversations in that bilious-walled attorney's room. Brown was far more searching in his questions than the District Attorney later was in court. He tried every device he knew, every trick and stratagem. He trapped Gibbs in lies about incidents which had occurred before the murder. Still he could not get the boy to change his version of the events at the Harnish cottage.

Brown pointed out that it was useless of Gibbs to attempt to protect anyone; that he was already in trouble, that he had brought grief to his parents, and that his wife had apparently turned against him.

The latter was true. Despite Helen Gibbs's promise to stick by her husband, she had retired to her parents' place near Sewell, New Jersey, hard by Pitman, and was not heard from again. Statements in her behalf were given out by her father and mother. She was not well, they said. She was confined to bed. Around Lancaster it was rumored that she had had a nervous collapse. People felt great sympathy for her. Some wrote letters telling her how they felt. Some wrote her letters urging her to pray.

Brown repeatedly told Gibbs that the jury might be more lenient if it was convinced that he was telling the truth. He told Gibbs, time and again, that his life was at stake. Gibbs continued to sit shaking his head. He never wavered, except when Brown proved that certain statements he had made about his past were lies. One of Brown's theories was that Gibbs might have killed the girl because he had propositioned her and she had threatened to tell Helen Gibbs. The lawyer had found out that Gibbs' behavior in the month before the crime was that of a sexually frustrated man, and he thought that if he could show knowledge of other extra-marital activities, Gibbs might be willing to go into the real details of his offense. Gibbs had vehemently denied that he had approached any other girls, but Brown had reason to believe he was lying.

In some instances Brown hires private investigators to collect evidence he needs, but in this case he and an associate, W. Roger Simpson, did their own detective

118

work. Brown had heard that Gibbs had borrowed a fellow student's car sometime after the Christmas holidays, and that he had used it to take out a girl who attended a school near Lancaster. Brown went out to Franklin and Marshall and contrived to learn the name of the girl. He and Simpson went to see her. She told them that the week before the murder Gibbs had called her to discuss a forthcoming Sigma Pi party; in the past, the girl had assisted fraternity committees in lining up dates for brothers and pledges, and Gibbs said he was hoping he could count on her co-operation again. Then he suggested that they might go to dinner at the Stockyards Inn the following Friday night to discuss it. The girl asked if Helen Gibbs would also be going along; Gibbs replied that she would. Helen Gibbs was then in Pitman. The girl agreed to the dinner date, but began worrying about it as soon as she put down the telephone. All day Friday she was ill. She tried unsuccessfully to get Gibbs on the telephone. Then she decided she simply could not go through with it. When Gibbs arrived to pick her up he found that she had left him a message saying she would be unable to go to dinner. In relating the incident to Brown and Simpson, the girl became hysterical; she was afraid her family might find out. Nevertheless, Brown gained her consent to testify in the event that he might deem it necessary.

Gibbs denied the episode. When Brown showed proof, he began to cry and admitted it; but he would not add anything to his story of the killing. Nor would he when Brown showed that he had been lying about another occurrence. This involved something which the Commonwealth later attempted to introduce as evidence at Gibbs' trial, but which the judge did not allow. The prosecution's version read, in part:

. . . the Commonwealth in rebuttal proposes to call M. E. C———, aged 19, ——— ——— Street, employed at the Armstrong Cork Company as a stenographer, who will testify that during the week of April 17th to 23rd, 1949, when the Fraternity had their Hell Week, and one of the restrictions placed on her boy friend, R. J———, was that he was not to see her, she was at home the entire week as part of the Easter vacation at McCaskey High School where she was a senior, Gibbs came to her home 3 times that week and stated that he was checking to see if J. was violating the Fraternity restriction; that he took her for a ride on all 3 occasions. The first time he drove her around town. The second time he drove her out near Bausman School where he turned off on the old road and parked. She objected to parking and he took her home. The third time, which she marked in her diary as being April 23rd, he drove her to a point near the Conestoga Country Club House and parked the car. He then asked her to move over to him, and when she asked why, he told her he wished to kiss her. Then he told her he loved her, wanted to divorce his wife and marry her, and asked her if she loved him. She told him she didn't and that he was silly. She also told him she wished to return home and he placed his head on the steering wheel and didn't say anything. He then drove her home, and enroute he asked her if she was going to tell his wife, and she said "No."

120

Brown's version of the story was substantially the same. Gibbs denied it, then admitted it. In court the prosecution had the girl standing by, ready to testify if called. The sight of her, according to Brown, upset Gibbs. "He seemed more worried about her being there," Brown later commented, "than he did about the fact that he was on trial for his life."

There was a corollary to the first incident which Brown failed to uncover. After receiving the note the girl had left, Gibbs had driven back to Lancaster. Around ten that night he turned up in The Rose Bowl, an Italian-style restaurant and bar on North Queen Street. The Rose Bowl on Friday and Saturday nights is crowded with young people. It is one of the few drinking places in the city where girls may go unescorted without endangering their good names. Young men and women who have no dates show up there, fall into convivial conversation, and leave in pairs, but the proprietors, Bruno and John Coluzzi, are strict as priests and allow no funny stuff on the premises. According to one girl, now married, Gibbs appeared slightly drunk when he came in. He approached several girls and suggested that they leave for some other spot. All refused. Finally he came to one girl he knew better than the rest, a pretty child who had recently married an acquaintance of his. He seemed excited when he saw that she was not with her husband. He sat down at her table.

"Where's Helen?" the girl asked.

"She took the car to Pitman to have it inspected," Gibbs said. "Say, how about going out to The Cabin?" (The Log Cabin, located about eight miles outside Lancaster on the road to Reading, is the most popular road-house among the younger people. Its proprietor, George

Leicey, and his wife, Anne, are as young as their clientele, and there is a Cabin "set" which has some of the aspects of a private club. Gibbs had never been a member of this group, but he felt that he was.)

"What are you driving, if Helen has the car?" the girl asked.

"I borrowed a convertible," Gibbs said. "Come on, we'll go see Anne and George."

"I don't think I'd better," the girl said.

"Come on," said Gibbs. "You're crazy about convertibles, aren't you? I know you are. You went around with C—— because of his convertible."

"That isn't true," the girl said indignantly.

"You did," Gibbs said. "You went out with him on account of his money and his convertible."

Gibbs was not joking or attempting to tease the girl. So great was his own respect for the trappings of success, and so successfully had his mind been invaded by the advertising-agency idea of what constitutes social acceptability, it was difficult for him to imagine one human being associating with another for reasons of simple warmth and companionship. Since he had a convertible, he could see no reason why the girl should not want to go out with him. He continued to urge her, and she still refused. Finally, as always happened, his temper broke.

"He was furious," the girl has recalled. "He went storming out of the place."

None of this came out at Gibbs' trial. Brown, today, is unable to decide what effect it might have had upon the jury's verdict. He doubts that evidence of Gibbs' sexual anxiety would have gained him the sympathy of the twelve. He is certain that only one factor might have aided the young man; he feels that it was unfortunate that Helen Gibbs chose not to sit in court while her husband was being tried. The actions of the wife have always puzzled him. Gibbs' mother had declared that Helen had said that she would stand by Eddie, but to Brown's almost certain knowledge Gibbs never heard from her. He wrote her several times (he told Brown) during his first few weeks in jail. He spoke of her often. She never answered. Gibbs sometimes wept when he thought about her. At one point, Brown attempted a ruse to get Helen to come to Lancaster. He told a reporter from a Philadelphia paper that he had it on good authority that the wife was planning to rally to her husband's side. The reporter published the statement; it was followed next day by an emphatic denial from Helen's mother. Brown now feels that he blundered. He believes that if he had had an opportunity to speak to Helen Gibbs, he might have persuaded her to co-operate.

Soon after meeting Gibbs, Brown decided that he had better enlist the aid of a psychiatrist; the more he spoke to the young man, the more he was convinced that he had gone out of his head when he killed Marian Baker. His friend and colleague, Thomas D. McBride, a well-known Philadelphia trial lawyer with whom he had collaborated in a number of cases, and whom he later called in for the Gibbs affair, suggested that he get in touch with Dr. Edward A. Strecker, Chairman of the Department of Psychology of the Under Graduate School of Medicine at the University of Pennsylvania, and a consultant to the Surgeon General of the Army. Dr. Strecker is one of the best-known psychiatrists on the Eastern seaboard; his testimony has been offered as evidence in countless trials. Dr. Strecker visited the Lancaster County prison twice and made two examinations of Gibbs, and also set into motion several other steps, including a neurological examination, an X-ray examination of Gibbs' skull, an electroencephalographic examination, and a Rorschach test, which was administered in Lancaster by Dr. Eleanor Ross, a qualified psychologist on the staff of the Institute of the Pennsylvania Hospital in Philadelphia. Gibbs was taken to Philadelphia for the other examinations. Dr. Strecker also made a fairly exhaustive inquiry into Gibbs's family background. At the same time, Brown ordered several other examinations, among them X-rays of Gibbs' sinuses and sella turcica, bladder area and external genitalia, as well as a blood serology test and an urinalysis.

Except for his refusal to change his story, Gibbs co-operated fully with his attorney. He answered all questions respectfully and turned over all personal papers and documents that Brown requested. In manner he was alternately cheerful and morose, but more the former than the latter. He seemed eager to digress from conversation about his crime at every opportunity, Brown recalls. He often spoke at length of his athletic exploits at Pitman High, retelling incidents in games in which he had distinguished himself. He was extraordinarily interested in baseball, and followed the progress of big-league teams closely. After his conviction in March, when Brown informed him that his case might not be settled until August or September or possibly later, he exclaimed joyfully, "Oh, boy! Maybe I'll get to hear the Series after all!" Warden Walter N. Foust has described Gibbs as a model prisoner. Warden Foust should know a model prisoner when one is in his charge; he has held his position twenty-eight years, and in 1953 ran for his fifteenth term (he is one of the few prison wardens in the United States who hold elective office; generally a warden is appointed). Gibbs' tenure at the jail was something of a trial for Warden Foust, who was often routed out of bed at three and four in the morning to answer inane questions long-distanced to him by

124

reporters in Chicago and other distant cities. He did not hold this against Gibbs. "The boy was a normal prisoner in every way," the Warden has recalled. "He was very co-operative . . . one of the high types. He was a very appreciative boy; anything anybody did for him, he appreciated it a lot." The Warden's official lack of emotion will not permit him to express his real feelings for Gibbs, but it is obvious that he felt sincerely sorry for him and may even have been fond of him. Nevertheless, he accorded him no special treatment or privilege. Gibbs was permitted the prescribed number of visits; he could be seen once each week, on Saturday, but by the same visitor only once each month. The exceptions to this were, of course, Brown and two ministers of the gospel, the Reverend Marvin Guice, of the Pitman Methodist Church, and the Reverend William Bollman, D.D., of the Lancaster First Reformed Church. Reverend Guice's presence is explained by his position as the Gibbs family minister. No one, including Reverend Bollman, who will not discuss Gibbs, has fully explained what *he* was doing there. A friend of Gibbs says that Edward once had heard Reverend Bollman preach a sermon and had been impressed, and that he asked the minister to come and see him. Reverend Bollman is well liked in Lancaster; he is known around town as a "regular" preacher. He is a husky, hearty man whose customary good humor does not altogether conceal his deep concern with matters of the spirit. One can easily imagine Gibbs, whose own father, according to all reports, had always been somewhat withdrawn and reticent by nature, coming to look upon the pastor as a kind of father-image or substitute. Under Reverend Bollman's guidance, Gibbs read many books on religion while in prison. It was later said that he planned, if he should be spared, to devote the large part of his time to religion.

125

Reverend Guice sent him a program of religious study and a first-step textbook. When Gibbs was not reading his Bible and the other material brought him by the ministers, he read the general run of magazines, comic books and newspapers supplied by the prison. He also read his mail, which was considerably heavier than that of most of the other inmates. He attempted to answer every letter faithfully, even some of the inevitable crank notes.

There was one girl in Lancaster who wrote him nearly every day. In one way, this girl symbolized the preoccupation with the case that many Lancastrians felt from the very moment of the announcement of Gibbs' arrest. No one has fully explained the fascination that the murderer held for the girl. She had known him only vaguely, having met him at Sigma Pi parties two or three times, and as far as anyone knows she had never been out with him except in the company of others. Neither the prosecution nor the defense found any reason to believe that she had ever met him clandestinely. Yet she wrote him letter after letter, some running to eight or nine pages. In gratitude, he had someone send her a little stuffed panda. On the night that he received his sentence, the girl retreated to her own room in her parents' house, where she held tightly to the toy and sobbed bitterly.

By the time the day of the trial arrived, Brown felt that he had done everything in his power by way of gathering information to bolster his case. He believed that he had a fifty-fifty chance of winning Gibbs a life sentence. He finally had become convinced, after his unceasing efforts to get Gibbs to elaborate, that the boy was telling what he believed to be the truth. He was unable to believe that Gibbs had consistent or chronic homicidal tendencies. He has said, "I used to think, sometimes, that if he *was* a murderer, or a maniac, he could easily have done me in

126

as we sat there in the attorney's room. But I honestly could never detect any real sign of irrationality in him. He was more intelligent than most clients, expressed himself well, and he had a good vocabulary. As far as I was concerned, I couldn't penetrate that analysis of Strecker's which we presented in testimony. I couldn't honestly say that Eddie Gibbs was any more abnormal than you or I." Brown had never before used psychiatric testimony in defending an accused murderer. Although he had come to trust Dr. Strecker, he was uneasy about the prospect of presenting the doctor's report simply because of his own unfamiliarity with the field. Today he says, without bitterness but with noticeable regret, "I wish I'd kept psychiatry out of the case. If I'd had my way completely, I'd simply have had Gibbs tell his story. The prosecution would never have introduced a psychiatrist if I hadn't brought one in first, and the verdict might have gone another way. Still, I don't know. The story Gibbs told doesn't make sense to a rational man. As each year passes I am more and more convinced he wasn't telling the whole truth."

Gibbs was arraigned on a charge of murder before Alderman J. Edward Wetzel on January twenty-eighth, a Saturday, at 10:00 A.M. Alderman Wetzel's office is located at 40 North Duke Street, on the west side of Lawyers' Row. Gibbs was led in by Constable Anthony Madonna. They were handcuffed together. Gibbs was wearing a windbreaker jacket, dungarees and loafers; his hair was mussed, but he was clean-shaven and he appeared calm and rested. There had been a brief preliminary hearing on January nineteenth, and because of it, Brown waived the reading of the murder charge. District Attorney John Milton Ranck took over the questioning from the alderman, whose day-to-day hearings are mainly concerned with traffic violations, drunkenness and disorderly

127

conduct, and disturbance of the peace. He called Deputy Coroner Dr. Charles P. Stahr, Corporal James E. Kane as Prosecutor, and Donald Mylin as Witness. Brown cross-examined Kane and Dr. Stahr but had no questions for Mylin. The testimony was substantially the same as that which was to come later in court. Throughout the hearing, which lasted less than a half hour, Gibbs showed little emotion. He sat staring at his feet, now and again touching the handcuffs dangling from his right wrist, occasionally touching his chin with the fingers of his left hand, as though to make certain of his own presence at this ritual which was so alien to anything in his previous experience. He did not appear to be nervous, reporters later said. He seemed annoyed at the photographers who were present, but not extremely so. When Brown finished his cross-examination of Corporal Kane, District Attorney Ranck said to Alderman Wetzel, "We request that you, on the basis of testimony produced, return this case to Court." Alderman Wetzel said, "The case of Edward Lester Gibbs is returned to the next term of Criminal Court, which will be held at Lancaster on Monday, March 13, 1950." Constable Madonna locked the handcuffs on his own wrist again and drew Gibbs outside to a car waiting to take him back to prison. A large crowd had gathered at the beginning of the hearing, and now it was larger. Some estimated it at nearly one thousand. Four policemen were sent over to keep order, but the crowd was undemonstrative. Gibbs did not appear to notice it. He kept his eyes averted as he stepped into the waiting car.

It may be that the silence of the people concealed a strong hostility. Many have said that public indignation never before had run so high in Lancaster. "There was a strong lynch-mob feeling in the town," Red Bricker, an *Intelligencer Journal* reporter and photographer, has recalled. "Lancaster isn't the kind of place that lynches anybody, but there were a lot around who were in favor of making a run on that jail and taking him out and stringing him up. I never saw anything like it around town." Part of the anger was unquestionably caused by Lancaster's indigenous suspicion toward outsiders; here, in the person of the murderer, was proof that they were not to be trusted. Part of it may have been stimulated by the brutality of the crime and its implications of sexual attack. And part of it may have been stirred by the local press. Brown, in later preparing an appeal for Gibbs, compiled a list of what he termed inflammatory material taken from the three Lancaster papers from January 13 to March 13, 1950. The list covers, in single-spaced typescript, twelve and one-half legal-sized pages.

Perhaps because he regarded himself as having been bidden by public sentiment, District Attorney John Milton Ranck took great pains in preparing the Commonwealth's case against Gibbs. He decided that he would appear in Court himself, the first time he had done so since his term had begun. The usual quota of local rancor accrued to him as a result of his decision; there were those, including some of his colleagues along the Row, who attributed it, and his subsequent brilliance in court, to political ambition. Ranck has not held public office since his retirement from the District Attorney's post in 1952. If he is looking to a political future, he thus far has kept his plans to himself. It is more plausible to assume that he was anxious to show the people of Lancaster that their law-enforcement officials were obsessed with a desire to see justice done.

Ranck is a conscientious man in the old-fashioned Lancaster County sense. He comes from one of the older and wealthier families in the section; his father, Milton Herr Ranck, of Strasburg, a hamlet to the east of the city, accumulated a respectable fortune in the tobacco business. Ranck attended public schools until his matriculation at Philips Exeter Academy, from which he graduated in 1928. He was Princeton '32 with an A.B. and took an LL.D. at the University of Pennsylvania in 1935. In Princeton he acquired the taste in clothes which has helped make him an object of rather breathless admiration to the Lawyers' Row female help. He is tall and lean, and wears business suits in the manner of a casual undergraduate; yet his frame is so constructed that the coats and trousers hang without fault or flaw. He affects short collars, or tab-collared shirts, which set off a handsome, strong-boned face. His dark hair and high forehead, his clean-shaven yet stubbornly black jowls, along with his dark eyes, lend his face something of the brooding quality of that of James Mason, the film actor. A Republican and a Presbyterian, Ranck is a director of the Hamilton Club, and he moves in the higher Lancaster social circles. His manner is one of extreme cordiality; he is an indefatigable nodder and greeter and smiler. There is nothing affected about the way in which he confronts the world; one can understand his having been that way all his life. He is forty-four. In 1938 he married the former Jean Howle, of Devonshire, England, who had come to Lancaster to visit a friend with whom she had gone to school in Switzerland. They have four young sons; they live in Ranck's native Strasburg.

At Princeton, Ranck starred on the track team as a pole-vaulter, and in 1930 he was a member of the combined Princeton-Cornell squad that went to England to take on Cambridge and Oxford. He went from Princeton to the University of Pennsylvania law school, and in 1935, after taking his degree and passing his state examinations, he went into the Lancaster office of John A.

130

Coyle. After Coyle died, Ranck shared offices with Daniel B. Strickler, now a General in the Army, and early in World War II, when Strickler was called to active military service, Ranck began looking after his local practice. When the Selective Service Act was passed, Ranck sat on a Lancaster County Board as government appeal agent. This Board held jurisdiction over an area in which there were Amish and Mennonites. Both sects are traditionally conscientious objectors, firmly opposed to military service of any kind. Early in 1944, after first attempting to get into the Marines as an enlisted man, Ranck was commissioned a second lieutenant. He was in Air Combat Intelligence and spent thirteen months in the Pacific, winding up in Japan. He and a small reconnaissance group were the first Americans into the atomic-bombed city of Nagasacki. In 1949, out of the service, Ranck and three other men, Roberts R. and Anthony Appel, and Herbert S. Levy, formed a partnership. They have done well. Ranck had become Second Assistant District Attorney in 1940; in 1944, he moved up to First Assistant, and he became District Attorney in 1948. It was the natural and usual progression in the city.

During Ranck's term, his Second Assistant was William Storb, a young man with a deceptively innocent-looking face. Storb is regarded as perhaps the most brilliant young lawyer in Lancaster; he is District Attorney as this is written. He is known for his incisive, loaded summaries, and his sarcasm; around the Row he is called "Snake-Tongued Willie." Ranck says it was Storb who handled the bulk of the work in getting the Commonwealth's case in shape for presentation. Storb says modestly that he did not; he says he merely assisted. The two had several disagreements, but not serious ones. Ranck was determined to make an issue of the garter belt Marian

Baker was wearing when she was killed. Because it had been pulled down, he wanted to make the jury believe that Gibbs had done it in an attempted sexual assault. Storb was dubious. So intent was Ranck upon proving this point that he sent his secretary, Catherine A. Baltasser, to buy him a garter belt of the same kind Marian Baker had worn. Ranck took the belt home and talked his wife into putting it on. He then dragged her around their living room late one night to find out if the undergarment and the outer clothing could have been disarranged in the same manner as Marian Baker's had been. Calling up Storb in excitement, he reported that he had verified his theory. Storb, between bursts of laughter, remarked that he was glad to hear it. The newspapers later reported that the police had conducted the same experiment with a "life-sized doll."

In any important case, it is the custom of both the defense attorney and the District Attorney to obtain from the courthouse the names of people called for jury duty and to make an investigation of each, so as to know whether to challenge or accept the individual when the trial begins and the jury is being selected. Ranck and Storb were especially meticulous in their examination of the individuals whose names had been drawn. The two men spent hours going over the photographs which had been taken of the Harnish cottage grounds and the victim's body. They finally picked fifty-seven which they planned to offer as evidence. "Our biggest problem," Storb said later, "was deciding what evidence to produce. We had so damned much of it."

When Brown asked permission to have Gibbs examined by Dr. Strecker, Ranck and Storb held a brief consultation and decided that they, too, would have to produce a psychiatrist who first would examine Gibbs and then, if his findings so indicated, testify as to his technically legally sane mind. As Brown had not, originally, neither Ranck nor Storb had seen any reason for bringing in psychiatry. "We wouldn't have introduced it if he hadn't," Ranck has said. He eventually got in touch with Dr. Baldwin L. Keyes, coincidentally enough a friend and colleague of Strecker and also a Philadelphian. Dr. Keyes had testified in many murder trials, but most often for the defense. His background was impeccable. He was Professor of Psychiatry at Jefferson Medical College in Philadelphia, and a consultant to both the Veterans' Administration and Philadelphia General Hospital. During World War II he had been a Colonel in the Medical Department of the United States Army. After Ranck had obtained permission from the court, Dr. Keyes went to Lancaster on March tenth and examined Gibbs in the Lancaster County Prison. Brown and Ranck exchanged copies of the reports the respective physicians had made, and each doctor helped his attorney to prepare a list of questions to ask the other attorney's doctor. As it happened, their disagreements were in degree, principally; and as it also happened, psychiatric testimony became a kind of legal football in the case, a deplorably frequent occurrence in this land of the suppressed desire.

Ranck was perhaps more optimistic than Brown as the date of the trial came nearer. He was ready to bet that he would win a conviction, but he was not so confident of gaining the death penalty. In the light of previous behavior of most Lancaster juries, he thought that too much to expect. He says, however, that he thought at the time, "If the jury won't hand down a death penalty in this case, why do we retain capital punishment in Pennsylvania?"

133

Edward Lester Gibbs was tried beginning Monday, March thirteenth, in the Court of Oyer and Terminer, General Jail Delivery, and Quarter Sessions of the Peace of Lancaster County. The formality of the Grand Jury, which sits for all cases before they are tried, was disposed of in fifteen minutes. The Grand Jury returned a true bill, and Gibbs was arraigned formally in Courtroom No. 1, before Judge Oliver S. Schaeffer, Presiding Judge, and Judge Joseph B. Wissler. It did not take long. Gibbs, wearing a tan suit and a figured necktie, stood with his hands folded before him, his eyes cast down, as the Court Clerk, Marian Lutz, read the charge, which said in part:

> "The Commonwealth charges that you, Edward Lester Gibbs, of Pitman, New Jersey, did on or about Tuesday, the 10th of January, A.D. 1950, in the County of Lancaster and the Commonwealth of Pennsylvania, near the summer cottage of Martin M. Harnish, in the Township of West Lampeter, Lancaster County, Pennsylvania, wilfully, feloniously, deliberately and premeditatedly, with malice aforethought, slay and kill a certain female person to wit: Marian Louise Baker, age 21 years, of 415 Reynolds Avenue, Lancaster City, Pennsylvania, by means of choking her and striking her in and about the head with a lug wrench, in violation of Sec. 701 of the Penal Code of 1939 contrary to the Act of Assembly of the Commonwealth of Pennsylvania in such cases made and provided . . . How say you?"

"Not guilty," said Gibbs, in a clearly audible voice. (Even though he had confessed to the murder of Marian Louise Baker, the law required that he plead "not guilty.")

134

"How do you wish to be tried?"

"By God and my country."

Presiding Judge Schaeffer ordered the trial removed to Courtroom No. 2. He assigned Judge Wissler to preside. Joseph B. Wissler, now sixty-one, was born in Clay Township in Lancaster County. He graduated from Lititz High, attended and graduated from Franklin and Marshall College, and was a member of the Class of 1916 at Harvard Law School. This sally into the world completed, he returned to his native County and became a practicing country lawyer. He served as District Attorney in Lancaster from 1924 to 1928. He has been judge in the Court of Common Pleas since 1942, and is regarded as a moderate, fair-minded man.

The veniremen were called at once. Ranck questioned each one first, asking each if he objected to capital punishment, if he had formed an opinion in the case, if this opinion could be changed, and finally, if he felt he could render an impartial verdict. From Ranck's tone and his questions, reporters concluded that he planned to ask for the death penalty.

When it came Brown's turn to question the prospect, he asked if the person had a fixed opinion on the penalty for first degree murder; if he had read "a lot of sensationalism" about the case; if he had daughters, and if so, what age; and finally, whether or not he had known either Marian Baker or Gibbs.

In all, 125 persons were interrogated before Ranck and Brown agreed upon the twelve jurymen and two alternates. In the morning the questioning went rather swiftly, but it began to drag in the afternoon; it occupied four hours and twenty minutes of the actual trial time. It provided the only bright spots of the entire event. They came mainly from jurors who answered sarcastically, aggressively, or whimsically. When Ira E. Mellinger, sixty-six, was called, the District Attorney asked the state of his health. "Just as you see it," said Mr. Mellinger. Ranck questioned him more closely, and the gentleman finally burst out, "I'm just as healthy as you and Mr. Brown!" He was dismissed. Later, when Robert Brighton, a bartender, was called, he declared that he always tried to agree with all his customers, no matter what they said. "One guy talks one way and one another," Brighton said. "I love to agree with them." He said it was up to a bartender to express both sides of any question, if he wanted to keep his customers. Ranck said, "We are not bartenders here." Brighton was dismissed amid laughter. Gibbs, at this point, brought his left hand suddenly to his face, as though to stop a smile. He smiled openly one other time—when the clerk called Mrs. Maude Gibbs, a waitress. That her name was the same as his apparently amused him. Throughout the day he sat almost motionless at the defense table, showing little of the nervousness his teachers in school had so often marked. Occasionally, however, he would fidget, now touching his lower lip, now his nose, now resting his chin on his cupped hands. A reporter in the *Lancaster New Era* wrote, "Most of the time he displayed a rather blank expression. At times he actually seemed bored with the proceedings as jurors were being picked."

The members of the jury were:
Mrs. Anna Kriwer, housewife, mother of two.
Walter T. Ferguson, farmer, father of six.
Mrs. Gertrude Dietrick, housewife, mother of two.
Russell K. King, clerk, married but childless.
Mrs. Margaret F. Bagger, housewife, mother of three.

Mrs. Helen Shirk, housewife, mother of two.

Paul S. Grimm, clerk, father of one.

E. Ellsworth Brandt, laborer, married but childless.

Mrs. Ruth Powlison, housewife, mother of two adopted children.

John E. Paes, farmer, father of two.

Charles L. Lee, manager of an electrical appliance store, married but childless.

The alternates were George S. Lantz, a retired employee of Armstrong Cork, married but childless; and Walter B. Aierstuck, Jr., a contractor, married but childless. Only five of the twelve jurors were from the city; both alternates were. The rest of them came from small county towns. Only two were college graduates, Mrs. Bagger and Mrs. Powlison. Each had gone to Vassar, and curiously enough, Mrs. Powlison had been a student in Mrs. Bagger's Psychology class when the latter taught there.

The jurors had a dreary time of it during the four days of the trial. Not only did their spines suffer the unrelenting chairs in their box all day, but at night they became virtual prisoners in Hotel Weber, across North Duke Street from the courthouse. There, locked in small and ancient rooms (the Weber is one of Lancaster's oldest hotels), they were denied newspapers and magazines and conversation with each other. They were not permitted radios, telephone calls, or communications from the outside. Their only contact with the outside world was through Charles Goos, tipstaff, who served as custodian for the men, and Mrs. Helen Hair, a registered nurse, who performed the same function for the women.

The trial began in earnest on Tuesday morning. The jurors came into court at nine twenty-five A.M., and Gibbs was brought in five minutes later. The papers noted "he looked more concerned than on the first day." At nine thirty-three, Judge Wissler entered. District Attorney Ranck stood up at once, and addressed the jury in his opening speech. After reading the indictment, he said, "It is now needless to state that this case is important to the defendant as well as to the Commonwealth."

Ranck then outlined, in some detail, the testimony he planned to produce. He concluded, "This defendant is charged with murder generally. The law in Pennsylvania says that if a jury finds someone guilty of first degree murder they have the option to set the punishment. This is the only crime in Pennsylvania in which the jury hands out the punishment."

He paused, ever so slightly.

"After you hear the evidence," he said, "I ask you to bring in a verdict of guilty . . . and I ask for the death penalty."

Ranck's first two witnesses were Corporal James Kane, who said that he had been sixteen years a State Policeman and that he was prosecutor in the case, and Officer Paul R. Schappert, who said he had been thirteen years with State Police, that his specialty was photographic work and fingerprinting, and that he had taken a bundle of photographs for the Commonwealth. When Ranck finished, Brown had no questions for either witness.

Now occurred the first of many sidebar conferences between Ranck, Brown and Judge Wissler. A sidebar conference is not entered in the official court records; it is an informal discussion between the attorneys and the judge on some point of law or procedure. In this first one, both attorneys requested that the photographs be examined for admissibility in Chambers. They requested this so that none of the photographs might be inadvertently seen by the jury. The jury was recessed, and the justice and the two counselors withdrew to the Judge's Chambers. There, their conversation was recorded in part as follows:

> MR. RANCK: I offer in evidence "Q.S. No. 1," a photograph showing the excavated portions under the building, two sheets of corrugated iron, two picnic table horses, two lawn mowers and two strips of beaver board.
>
> MR. BROWN: No objection.
>
> THE COURT: Admitted.
>
> MR. RANCK: I offer in evidence "Q.S. No. 2," a photograph showing the entrance to the men's room in the rear of Erb's Service Station located in East Lampeter Township . . . where the ring, property of Marian Louise Baker, was found.
>
> MR. BROWN: No objection.
>
> THE COURT: Admitted.
>
> MR. RANCK: I offer in evidence "Q.S. No. 3," a photograph showing a partial view of the body of Marian Louise Baker after she had been turned over on her back, and shows the front of the body and how the clothing were disarranged.
>
> MR. BROWN: That is objected to.
>
> THE COURT: The objection is overruled.
>
> MR. RANCK: I offer in evidence "Q.S. No. 4," a photograph showing a view of the back of Marian Louise Baker, before she was moved.
>
> MR. BROWN: That is objected to. As to "Q.S. No. 3" and "Q.S. No. 4" I think I should state the basis of my objection . . . [they are] objected to as being pictures that are not necessary to be shown to the jury for the purpose of

proving the Commonwealth's case, showing in both instances the position of the body, and which pictures can be described by oral testimony by witnesses for the Commonwealth sufficiently to fully acquaint the jury with the place at which the body was found and the position in which it was, and further, because the showing of these . . . will only tend to inflame the emotions of the jury to the prejudice of the defendant. I might add, as to "Q.S. No. 3," I have the further objection that this picture does not show the position in which the body was found, but shows a picture of the body after it had been turned over. I object, further, because all the facts that this exhibit would tend to prove can be proved by testimony without the use of photographs which tend to excite the emotions of those who view them.

MR. RANCK: It is very important to the Commonwealth's case that "Q.S. No. 3" be admitted in evidence. It has a bearing on the manner in which the body was dragged by the defendant, and the position and condition of her clothing as shown . . . forms an integral part of our case.

THE COURT: Objection overruled.

MR. BROWN: My objections as to inflaming the minds of the jury on subsequent photographs will be the same as they were to "Q.S. No. 3" and "Q.S. No. 4."

Ranck offered another view of the body before it had been moved; Brown objected, and was overruled. Then Ranck offered a view of the ground which the Harnish family used as a dump, to show where the defendant had attempted to dig a grave for the body. Brown had no objection.

The next photograph showed Gibbs pointing to the corduroy jacket which he had removed from its place of concealment beneath the flooring in the attic of East Hall. Brown objected to this and was sustained. Two similar pictures followed and were ruled out. Ranck produced a view of the excavation under the Harnish cottage, and it was admitted over Brown's objection. So was the next, which showed Gibbs pointing to the spot where he had committed the murder. A photograph showing Gibbs indicating where he had parked his car to dispose of Marian Baker's umbrella and pocketbook and the lug wrench was not admitted, but Ranck was permitted to use one of Gibbs holding the shovel he had used to attempt to bury the victim's body. Pictures of Marian Baker's umbrella being removed from the Little Conestoga Creek, and of Gibbs pointing to the spot in the creek where he had disposed of her pocketbook, were offered, objected to, and ruled inadmissible.

> MR. RANCK: I offer . . . "Q.S. No. 16," showing the upper part of the body . . . after the two large sheets of corrugated metal and the wooden horses had been removed. I might say, if the Court please, this is a picture of the actual scene of the uncovering of the body, and we think it important.
>
> MR. BROWN: Objected to . . . on the grounds . . . that the facts . . . can be proved by testimony without the use of photographs, and tend to excite the emotions of those who view it.

THE COURT: You are offering this for the purpose of showing the concealment of the crime?

MR. RANCK: Yes.

THE COURT: It is allowed for that purpose. Objection overruled.

Now Ranck held up a picture of a rake removing Marian Baker's pocketbook from the creek; it was refused. So was one showing Gibbs pointing to a spot on the Harnish property where he had dragged the body, and one showing Sergeant Simpson removing a lug wrench from the Little Conestoga. A picture of Gibbs showing where he had hidden the body was then admitted. Several more were ruled out in rapid succession: one showing him pointing to the spot where he had thrown the lug wrench, one showing where he had thrown the pocketbook before putting it in the creek, one showing another view of the spot where he had attempted to bury the body, one showing where he had thrown the umbrella, and two showing him pointing to the excavation under the cottage.

MR. RANCK: I offer in evidence "Q.S. No. 28," which is a close-up of the head as the body was found. You can see the leaves around her shoulders. You can see the injury to the head.

MR. BROWN: Objected to on the grounds that it is a picture that can be testified to, and which will tend to inflame the minds of the jury.

MR. RANCK: This is a photograph of the body before it was touched.

THE COURT: The objection is overruled.

A view of the area through which Gibbs dragged the body, two views of the cottage, a second view of the back of Marian Baker's wounded head, a view of her back and left side, and another view of the drag mark were ruled out. Then the Judge admitted over Brown's objection a general view of the cottage and the drag mark.

Ranck's next photograph was a particularly grisly close-up of the head when the body was found. It showed the injuries to the head clearly. Brown objected heatedly to this picture, but was overruled.

The remaining photographs were disposed of in rapid-fire order. Those which the Judge admitted included a general view of the cottage and the drag mark, a shot showing how Gibbs had spread leaves about in an attempt to conceal his deed, views of the front and south sides of the cottage (showing the drag marks again), a view of the rear of Gibbs' car (to show where he had removed the lug wrench), a view of the water pump, a second one from another angle, and two more of Marian Baker's body. The Judge would not admit eight more photographs showing the wounds on the face and skull; he said, "The Court feels there have been sufficient photographs already identified, and admitted."

The conference in Chambers took one hour and forty minutes. While the court was recessed, Gibbs had continued to sit at the counsel table. Observers noted that he was much more jittery than he had been the day before. At one point he picked up a glass of water and swallowed what the newspapers described as "a nerve pill." The *New Era* report said, "[He] nervously played with his fingers, twitching them one by one." Almost directly behind him sat his father and the Reverend Marvin Guice. His mother did not attend any sessions of the trial, but several of Marian Baker's relatives did.

When the session resumed, Ranck called Edgar M. Sachs, a photographer employed by the Lancaster *New*

143

Era. Ranck showed him an aerial view of the Harnish cottage, and Sachs said that he had taken it on Sunday, January fifteenth. Brown cross-examined him only to find out the name of the pilot of the plane, which was George Ritnour. Ranck offered the photograph as "Q.S. No. 56," and it was admitted.

Mrs. Martin M. Harnish was called. She identified her cottage from the photographs and told how she had found the body. The jury appeared to be exceptionally interested in what she had to say. Brown cross-examined her briefly to no apparent effect. Dr. Charles P. Stahr then took the stand and testified as to finding the body, examining it, and removing it to the hospital. Brown cross-examined him briefly, in part as follows:

Q—Now, Doctor, you described the injuries. I don't think you said you found abrasions on the body, or anything of that character?

A—I hadn't stated that.

MR. RANCK: I didn't ask the doctor to testify as to marks on the body. I asked him what was the cause of death. We will go into that later.

Q—Well, how thorough an examination did you make there at the scene other than what you explained?

A—No, I didn't examine the body of the deceased at the scene. I simply examined the head.

Q—You did testify [as to the examination of the body] at the preliminary hearing, but you didn't hear today?

A—That was my examination at the hospital.

144

Q—Who assisted you in the conduction of that examination?

A—Dr. Heid.

MR. BROWN: All right. That is all, Doctor.

Donald Mylin was sworn. He said that he had been treasurer of Franklin and Marshall five years and that Marian Louise Baker had worked for the college about four. He described her duties. He told what had happened the day she disappeared, and what occurred the next morning and afternoon when he gave the alarm. Then he told about identifying her body. Under cross-examination, he said that she sometimes brought sums of money back from the bank after she had deposited checks, and that on such occasions he always took her to the bank in his car and brought her back. Mrs. Nancy Stonesifer was next called. She described Marian's activities on the morning of the day she disappeared, up until the time she had left the office to go downtown. She described her clothes minutely, and her purse and umbrella. Brown got up to object to the line of questioning. Ranck said:

I am offering by this witness an identification of the clothing that was worn by the victim on the day of her disappearance and subsequently removed from her body at the morgue . . .

MR. BROWN: It is objected to on the ground that the District Attorney has already stated in his opening remarks that he intends to prove a confession on the part of the defendant that he killed this Marian Baker, and that the bringing out here of what kind of clothing she had on and what kind of an umbrella she carried is not relevant and not necessary to the proof of the Commonwealth's case, and unduly prolongs the trial of the case, and tends to inflame the emotions of the jury by bringing out unnecessary details.

MR. RANCK: If the Court please, the umbrella, according to the confession . . . was torn apart, and the cloth material weighted with a stone and thrown into the Little Conestoga Creek. The ribs of the umbrella were torn apart and thrown into the Creek. The handbag of the victim, after the removal of $14.00, was torn apart, a hole put in the bottom and a stone inserted, and was thrown into the same Little Conestoga Creek to secrete and conceal evidence.

MR. BROWN: The objection is withdrawn.

Ranck showed Mrs. Stonesifer the remnants of Marian Baker's purse and umbrella. She identified them, and they were admitted as evidence with no objection from Brown.

Percy LeRoy Campbell, the post office clerk who had waved to Marian Baker as she passed his window, was called. He told of his last sight of her.

Mrs. Hope Renninger, the bank clerk, told of her last conversation with Marian Baker.

Dr. George Joseph Heid, Jr., told in detail of the autopsy he had performed on Marian Baker's body. During his testimony, Ranck produced Marian Baker's garter belt and pants, marked "Q.S. No. 59," and "Q.S. 60," respectively. Sidebar, he said:

I offer to show by this evidence that in the course of performing the autopsy . . . he had occasion to remove the clothing . . . He removed a garter belt from which 2 eyelets, together with the material to which they are attached, have been ripped. If the Court please, I direct . . . attention to "Q.S. No. 3," being a view of the anterior portion of the thighs. The Court will note protruding below the pants which have been described the end of a garter belt. This . . . is in a torn condition. I especially call . . . attention to the fact that the eyelets where this particular garter belt were obviously hooked have been ripped from the material, and that subsequent evidence will disclose where one of these eyelets was found. We feel that this evidence is an extremely important portion of the Commonwealth's case, as will be brought out in argument to the jury, as to what motions this defendant made or possibly made to this victim prior to the killing. It is tied in with the method of dragging this body which will clearly demonstrate these eyelets were not ripped out by virtue of the dragging, and were, therefore, ripped out by some other force, and we wish to argue to the jury what force that may have been. For that reason we believe that both the garter belt and pants, which, if the Court please, physical examination will show have elastic at the top and around each leg and kept the torn garter belt in position so that it could not fall to the ground, are important. The Commonwealth offers . . . the garter belt, for the purpose of showing possible motive.

MR. BROWN: We contend that the only relevant testimony here is the testimony with regard to blows on the head which Dr. Stahr said caused the death. Now, to bring in clothing, underwear, brassiere, skirt, etc., without any proof there was any attack or rape or anything like that is irrelevant, immaterial, and incompetent, and is inclined to inflame the minds of the jury. We therefore object to this.

THE COURT: Objection overruled.

Both the pants and the garter belt were admitted as evidence. Dr. Heid went on describing his autopsy. When he had finished, Brown began an attempt to discredit Ranck's case before the latter could get it underway:

Q—Doctor . . . you testified that the skirt was turned upward; is that right?

A—Yes, sir, upward over the thorax.

Q—Did that come from dragging?

A—It could very well come from dragging.

Q—Describe what you mean by up over the thorax.

A—Up over the chest and umbilica, that is the belly button, if I may use a common word, was exposed.

Q—We prefer you to use common terms. That was exposed by reason of the dress being turned up?

A—Yes, sir.

*

Q—Where was the garter belt?

A—That garter belt was partly covering the front of the right and left upper leg, that is, the thighs.

Q—Under the pants?

A—It had been pulled down partway. The

148

upper portion was underneath the low margin of the pants and the lower part had been pulled down . . .

Q—That could have been caused by dragging, too?

A—If someone had pulled the strap.

Q—But if the body was being dragged along the ground?

A—If the body were being dragged by the feet it would seem the garter belt would be thrust in the opposite direction.

Q—But if it were dragged in the opposite direction?

A—By the shoulders? That could be, mechanically, yes.

Q—And the pants were intact, were they not?

A—They were intact so far as I could determine.

*

Q—You didn't find any outward trauma on the body?

A—Not on the chest or abdomen.

*

Q—Will you describe what you call the genitals?

A—. . . The vagina, uterus, cervix, ovaries, oviduct.

Q—Was an examination of those made?

A—. . . Microscopically.

Q—Entirely undamaged?

A—Undamaged, correct, as far as I could determine.

Q—Was there any outward visible indication of any damage by violent entrance?

A—No.

Q—And was there any indication of any sexual relationship?

MR. RANCK: Objected to.

THE COURT: Objection overruled.

A—I couldn't determine whether sexual relations had been performed.

*

Q—Did you see any evidence of any violence?

A—Around the genitalia?

Q—Yes.

A—No.

Q—None, whatsoever?

A—No.

Brown next attempted to find out if dragging could have caused some of Marian Baker's hand injuries. The Doctor said he doubted it; they had probably come from blows. Brown turned to the garter belt.

Q—Was that garter belt . . . completely around the deceased's body?

A—No, sir, it was loosened. We saw the attachments. They were visible . . . when the body was on the table.

Q—How much of it was not around the body, approximately?

A—Well, it was pulled forward. That is the best I can do. I would say it was about 50% around the body. I am just estimating.

Q—Altogether under the pants?

A—No. The lower edge was beneath the lower border of the pants on each side.

Ranck came back to question the pathologist. He concentrated on the sizes of the holes in Marian Baker's skull. Dr. Heid described them minutely. Brown then returned and got the Doctor to testify that he had found no evidence of rape. He said that he had been able to find no spermatazoa, but they after all usually undergo dissolution after from six to twelve hours in a dead body. He concluded his testimony by stating that in his opinion Marian Baker was alive when some of the blows were struck.

John K. George, twenty, of Greensburg, Pennsylvania, a sophomore at Franklin and Marshall, was called. After putting these facts about him into the record, Ranck said:

Q—Now, will you state what happened in the early afternoon of Tuesday, January 10th, 1950, with reference to this defendant, Edward Lester Gibbs?

A—Well, Ed and I left the Fraternity House at approximately 1:30, quarter of 2:00 . . . drove in Ed's car down town and we parked the car behind the post office on that street, I am not sure of the name of it, but it runs behind . . . We left the car there, went up to Queen Street by the Pennsylvania Hotel and went over to the Hamilton Theatre. The ticket booth wasn't open yet. We walked around, loafed around the town to wait and see when it was going to open. It did finally open, I am not sure what the time was, but we purchased our tickets for the movies and a fellow standing behind the ticket booth informed Ed the picture had been pulled and the ones scheduled to be shown would not be shown, and they wouldn't have a replacement until quarter of 3:00.

Q—Do you remember the picture originally advertised to be shown that day?

A—I don't remember the name, sir; no.

Q—Well, what happened when you found out that information, learned that information?

A—Eddie said to me he didn't have time to see this picture since he had to pick up his wife at Armstrong's at 5:00 o'clock, so he gave the tickets back to the lady and got the money back and we went out in front of the Hamilton Theatre and were talking for a while, a couple of minutes, five minutes, maybe, and I hadn't seen the picture at the Colonial Theatre . . . I borrowed a dollar off Ed to go to that picture because it was the last day and I hadn't seen that movie . . . He had seen it earlier in the week.

MR. BROWN: That is the picture at the Colonial?

THE WITNESS: That is right.

Q—Did you see Eddie that night? When did you next see Eddie Gibbs?

A—That night.

Q—Just tell what happened.

A—I had gone over to the apartment like I had many other nights, after dinner at the Fraternity House. When I first got there Ed wasn't there, but his wife was, so I sat down and we talked, I guess I don't remember for sure. Ed came in a little later—I am not sure of the time of that either—and he was sweated up a bit, and I believe it was Helen who asked him, his wife asked him where he had been and he said, "Over in the gym shooting basketball."

Q—Shooting?

A—Basketball.

George then related how Gibbs later tried to establish an alibi for that afternoon, and how, later, he had told him that he was going to the President's office to confess. Brown took over. He made George go over his previous testimony in an attempt to ascertain the time the two had gone to the movies.

Max Hannum took the stand and testified as to Gibbs's manner of turning himself over to the authorities. Dr. Theodore A. Distler was called for corroboration. Brown had no questions for either.

Corporal James Kane took the stand, recalled by Ranck. Now the actual details of the murder, as the Commonwealth saw them, were to come out at last. Ranck began questioning his witness slowly. He first had Kane tell about his investigation of the murder scene, verifying the photographs which had been admitted as evidence. He told of examining the condition of Marian Baker's garter belt, pants, and stockings, and he described the drag marks at length. He said that an eyelet had been found, and Ranck offered it as evidence. It was admitted over Brown's objection. Marian Baker's smashed watch was exhibited and identified and admitted. Then Ranck led the officer around to telling what had happened the day he and Detective Matt had taken Gibbs into custody. Kane described the scene in Hannum's office briefly, and then continued:

. . . At 4:45 Mr. Hannum entered his office and had with him this defendant. He said,

"This is Edward Gibbs. He has something to tell you." Edward Gibbs said, "I am the fellow you are looking for. I killed Marian Baker." . . . he started to cry, sat down, and said, "Do I have to go to the electric chair?" He then made a disconnected statement to the effect that "I am an intelligent fellow. I have almost completed my college course. I thought I could get away with this and beat the rap. I scattered things around and I don't think you could ever find them." I asked him what he had used to kill Marian Baker and he told me a lug wrench from his car. I asked him what he had done with the lug wrench and her personal effects and he told me he had taken them out and put them in a stream back of Maple Grove Park, that he had taken her rings and placed them in the toilet in the men's room of a gas station just East of the City of Lancaster. At that time I called our barracks by phone. Mr. Gibbs continued to talk to Detective Matt, and I don't know exactly what was said. However, I did hear him say he had had an alibi built up with a friend of his who had gone to the movies. He then offered to take us out to the stream. . . . I went to get the car. . . . He directed me to a point along the Little Conestoga Creek about one-fifth of a mile South of Route 30, just West of Lancaster, told me where to park the car, and said that is where he parked his. . . . He then . . . pointed out three different places along the Creek, designating the first one as the point where he had disposed of the lug wrench, the second spot where he had disposed of the pocketbook, and

154

the third where he had disposed of the umbrella. . . . He stated that previous to throwing the pocketbook into the stream he had removed $14.00 from the wallet he had found in the pocketbook, had torn a hole in the pocketbook so it wouldn't float, placed a stone in it and then threw it in the water, that he had ripped the cover from the umbrella, wrapped it around a piece of stone and thrown that in the stream, and had also bent the frame of the umbrella and threw that in at the same point he had thrown the cover in. He said he had also thrown the handle into the stream, but as I recall it, it was in the middle of the stream, and he felt we wouldn't recover it. He said he had also thrown his clothes, consisting of a pair of socks, sweater and jacket into the stream at the same point he disposed of the wrench, but the following day he had gone back, found the clothing was still floating at the same point, had removed it from the stream, took it back to East Hall . . . where he concealed it under the attic floor. We then re-entered the automobile and started toward the barracks. He had conversation with Detective Matt . . . and I didn't hear all of his remarks. He did repeat, however, something about having an alibi, said he was intelligent, and reminded me there were several other unsolved murders in the State, spoke of the one which occurred at State College, at which time I asked him if he knew Rachel Taylor, which was a victim, and a resident of New Jersey, and he said he didn't. He referred to the moving picture he was going to see that day as being a sex picture and said he felt the reason the picture wasn't shown was because of Dr. Spotts, I believe, who was a member of the Franklin and Marshall faculty, and Mr. Gibbs said Mr. Spotts is responsible, or has been responsible for a number of movies being withdrawn in Lancaster.

Brown stood up quickly. "I move that part of the testimony where he talks about sex and movies and Spotts be stricken from the record."

Assistant District Attorney William Storb got to his feet. "That goes to show motive, the state of mind of this defendant, shows he was in a sexy mood."

The motion was overruled by the Court.

Ranck bade Kane continue with his story. Kane said:

Somewhere during that ride . . . Detective Matt warned Gibbs that anything he might say would be used against him. . . . Mr. Gibbs said, "I know all about that, but it is a relief to get it off my mind. I can't eat, I couldn't sleep, I am very conscious of the scratch on my face, and every time I talk to people I cover it up." In discussion of the actual murder, evidently in response to a question asked by Detective Matt, he said, "I thought she would never die." There were other remarks made . . . but I didn't hear them all. We arrived at the barracks at approximately 5:30, and approximately one hour later we started to take a written statement . . .

The statement, three and one-third single-spaced typewritten pages long, was exhibited, shown to have been witnessed by State Police officers, and read into the record. Parts of it went as follows:

"Edward we are investigating the murder of Marian Louise Baker and you have been taken into custody because you have admitted the commission of this crime. You are now informed that you have the right to refuse to answer any or all questions which may be asked you and further that any statement you may make can be used against you in the event of a trial. . . . Under these circumstances are you willing to make a statement relative to what occurred?

"A—Yes I am willing to tell you.

"Q—Tell me in your own words all that you know about this crime.

"A—I ate lunch at the college coffee shop with John George, Bob Gibb and George Annis. We left there and went back to the Sigma Pi Fraternity House and remained there for about one hour and a half. John George and I decided to go to the Hamilton to the movies. When we arrived there we discovered they were not going to show the movies they advertised, so we walked up Queen Street as far as the Square and back down to Chestnut Street as far as the smoke shop and then back to the Hamilton. At this time the movie was open. I bought the tickets. The fellow said the show wasn't going to start until a quarter to three and I decided it was too late for me to go. I got my money back and went out in front of the Hamilton and John decided to go see "On the Town" which was at the Colonial. I left him and started to go to the Grand. I changed my mind and came back to the same side of Queen Street. I met Marian Baker in front of the Western Union. I asked her if she was going back to the College and she said 'As soon as I mail a letter.' I told her I would meet her in front of the Post Office and I went down to the Farmer's Arcade Market and got my car, drove in front of the Post Office and Marian came across and got in the car. I asked her if she was in a hurry to get back to the College and she said, 'No,' so I took a left on Prince Street and went right straight out Prince, as far as Media Heights Golf Course, turned left and went past Media Country Club. We drove all the ways back as far as Rocky Springs, came out again past Media Country Club and took a left and drove on up 222, took a left in the lane, or road, went all the way back to where the drive makes a circle. I stopped the car, reached over and choked her. She screamed and got out of the car and I chased her. She didn't get very far. I continued choking her. Then I went and got the keys out of the car and opened it up and got the lug wrench. I hit her with it, I don't know how many times. I pulled her body down below the knoll by the garbage pile, threw her pocketbook away, not too far, and got back in my car and drove back to the College, went in, got undressed, took a shower, then I came back to my room and got dressed. Took the coat, sweater and socks and put them in the back seat of the car and then drove back out to where Marian was. I picked up her pocketbook and left. Went out behind Maple Grove [*an amusement park on the western edge of the city—RG*] and threw the lug wrench, my coat, socks and sweater, her pocketbook and umbrella in the stream and left and went back to the College. Went to Armstrong and picked up my wife. Went to dinner at the Y.M. and back to College. About 7:30 I went out again. I took the shovel from the basement of East Hall and drove out to where Marian was again. Tried to dig grave down by the garbage pile but the roots prevented me. I started looking around and found a place under the cottage. I dragged the body up there and put the corrugated tin and horse over it, scattered some

158

leaves around it and put the incinerator over by it and left. Went out to Stumpf's Service Station and got rid of the rings, continued out to Van Brocklin's [*a student whose wife was to have typed a paper for Gibbs—RG*] and came back to the College where I remained the rest of the night. I went out the next day and got the jacket out of the stream behind Maple Grove, brought them back and hid them under the floor boards, in the attic of East Hall.

"Q—How did you travel from F. & M. College to the movies?

"A—Automobile.

"Q—Whose automobile?

"A—Mine.

*

"Q—What conversation did you have with Marian Baker enroute to the cottage?

"A—She was saying something about the College, but I don't recall what it was. However, I do recall that as we went over the bridge at Engleside, I said the tires sound good, they were singing.

"Q—Did you see anyone you knew from the time Marian got in the car until you left her at the cottage?

"A—Not to my knowledge.

"Q—You have stated that after you dragged Marian down to the garbage pile you threw her pocketbook away. Where was the pocketbook?

"A—It was back up at the spot where I hit her.

"Q—Where was the lug wrench you used to strike Marian?

"A—In the trunk of the car. That's one thing I forgot to tell you. I went out to Bob Hesses and bought a new lug wrench.

"Q—How long did you choke Marian before she stopped resisting?

"A—I have no idea. It could have been three or four minutes, but in a situation like that time is the furtherest thing from your mind.

*

"Q—When did you remove the money from Marian's pocketbook?

"A—I took the money out of it when I threw it, when I threw it into the stream.

"Q—How much money did you remove from the pocketbook?

"A—$14.00.

"Q—In what denominations, and do you have any of it left?

"A—Ten and four ones, and No, I don't have any of it left.

"Q—What did you do with the wallet and other articles which were in the pocketbook?

"A—All the articles were in the pocketbook. I ripped a hole in it, put a rock in it so it wouldn't float, and threw it in the stream.

"Q—Did you throw all the articles in the stream at the same place?

"A—No; I threw the lug wrench in first; about 25 feet downstream I threw the pocketbook in; then I broke up the umbrella and threw it in about 30 feet downstream.

"Q—When did you remove the rings from Marian's fingers?

"A—The last trip at night.

"Q—Why did you take the rings?

"A—I just don't know.

"Q—You have stated that you scattered some leaves around after you concealed the body. . . . Why did you do this?

"A—I just don't know.

"Q—Did you place the leaves there in order that any person who would look at the corrugated iron would not think it had been moved recently?

"A—I guess that's what went through my mind. I don't remember.

*

"Q—Did you have a flashlight when you returned to the cottage for the third time?

"A—Yes, I did.

*

"Q—Will you describe this flashlight for me and tell me where it is at the present time?

"A—It's black, an Eveready, with silver ends. It is down at my father-in-law's in South Jersey. . . . I didn't have a flashlight before and I didn't want to cast suspicion upon myself by having one all of a sudden. . . . That's another thing I forgot to tell you. There are so many things going through my mind I forgot to tell you about it. I purchased it at a small grocery store on Prince Street on my way out to the cottage that night for the purpose of light.

*

"Q—I now show you a yellow gold ring, containing six small diamonds and one larger diamond which was recovered from the toilet at Stumpf's gas station today and ask you if you recognize this as one of the rings you removed from Marian's finger?

"A—Looks like it. I didn't examine it too closely, but I know it was a diamond ring.

"Q—What did you spend the money for which you took from Marian's pocketbook?

"A—I don't remember. I just put it in with my own money and spent it.

"Q—Edward, how have you been treated since you were taken into custody?

"A—Very fine. It couldn't have been any better.

"Q—Why did you make this statement?

"A—Things build up in you when you do a terrible thing like I have done, it just builds up inside you. It's not human to keep it inside you."

Marian Baker's engagement ring was admitted as evidence, and Corporal Kane told how he and the other officers took Gibbs to the office of J. Edward Wetzel, an Alderman, to swear to the truth of his statement. After that, Kane continued, they took Gibbs to the scene of the crime, where he re-enacted it, to the Little Conestoga Creek behind Maple Grove, and to East Hall where he procured the shovel he had used in attempting to dig a grave for his victim. The shovel was admitted as evidence. Kane said:

> . . . we went to the attic where Edward Gibbs pointed out the section of the attic floor under which he had concealed his jacket. He was photographed while doing that. I reached under the floor and I found a brown corduroy jacket. I was then taken to another section of the floor and he pointed that out as being the place where he had concealed his sweater, and I reached under the floor and recovered a thin knitted sweater. We continued to search for his socks but were unable to find them that evening. . . . The following morning Sgt. Simpson, Detective Matt, Cpl. Jenkins and Pvt. Miller, from Harrisburg, who came here with

an electric magnet, went to the Little Conestoga Creek and we recovered the lug wrench, the pocketbook with contents, the umbrella cover—

Ranck produced these objects, questioned Kane to ascertain that they were the ones of which he was speaking, and the Court admitted them as evidence. The District Attorney then sought to show that Gibbs had later made statements about his offense which were not included in his written confession. Kane speaking:

On February 4th together with the Lancaster County Sheriff, Abe Lane, Pvt. Paul Oreszko, of the State Police, and Sgt. Simpson, of the State Police, I transported the defendant to the Philadelphia General Hospital in order that he might undergo examination and tests. Enroute to Philadelphia he told me that after thinking it over he recalled that he had said he purchased a new lug wrench at the Hess Motor Company on East King Street, of Lancaster, that he had been in error, that he really purchased it at Wiggins Motor Company, on the Harrisburg Pike. He also stated he had forgotten to tell me the real reason he returned to the scene of the crime the second time was this: that after killing Marian Baker he attempted to wash the blood from his hands at a pump which is located near the cottage. He was unable to get any water out of the pump, and after returning to the College he realized he might have left his fingerprints on the pump handle and he had not left the pump handle in the position in which he found it, that he obtained a Turkish towel from his bedroom, returned to the scene, wiped the pump handle and placed it in the original position where it was secured by a wire.

A photograph of the cottage and the pump was shown, and Court adjourned until 9:30 A.M. the following morning, when Brown began his cross-examination of Kane. Brown had had a bad night; the impact of the police officers' testimony had worried him all during the previous day. Now he was edgy, and his questions were couched in a sharp voice. He was trying to show that the officers had botched the statement they had taken from Gibbs, and that the Commonwealth was trying to get admitted as evidence things which Gibbs had said to the officers in conversation. He interrogated Kane closely on the Gibbs statement, and then he suddenly switched to Kane's testimony of the previous day, the part where Kane had said that Gibbs had said, "I am an intelligent fellow. I thought I could get away with this and beat the rap. I scattered things around and I don't think you could ever find them." Brown speaking:

> Q—Now, officer, you talked to Gibbs, as I understood you to say yesterday, at some length coming in from the college campus to the barracks?
>
> A—No, sir, the only conversation was between Detective Matt and Gibbs. I only asked him one question.
>
> Q—All right, whether it was between you or not, you were in the front seat and he and Detective Matt were on the back seat?
>
> A—Yes, sir.
>
> Q—When was this conversation supposed to have taken place that you gave yesterday that either was said to Matt, or said in your hearing,

164

that she was hard to kill, and she didn't want to die?

A—He made the remark he thought she would never die, or she didn't want to die, in the car.

Q—Coming to the barracks?

A—Yes, sir.

Q—Why didn't you put that in the written statement?

A—It was just an oversight.

Q—It was an oversight?

A—Yes, sir.

Q—A matter you are making so much moment of now, you call an oversight in not having it in his statement?

A—There was a considerable amount of information contained in the statement. I just overlooked it.

Q—Officer, you look at this statement. You see three pages, or 2½ pages of questions and answers?

A—Yes, sir.

Q—Short questions and answers?

A—Yes, sir.

Q—And for the first time yesterday in this entire proceeding you divulged the fact that he was supposed to have made that remark, didn't you?

A—Yes, sir.

Q—Isn't it a fact he didn't make any such remark?

A—I overheard him making that remark to Detective Matt.

Q—Didn't that register as an important

and damaging statement of the defendent to you?

A—He was talking almost constantly. It did register in my mind.

Q—I am asking you the question, didn't that register as an important and damaging statement of the defendant to you?

A—Yes, sir, at the time.

Q—And yet you don't have it in this signed statement?

A—No, sir.

Q—And you call it an oversight?

A—Yes, sir.

Both Ranck and Storb were concerned by this line of questioning; they felt that Brown had scored tellingly for the first time. Yet Kane remained doggedly unshaken. Brown determined to crack his resistance and to again shake the jury's confidence in the reliability of the witness. He proceeded to examine him minutely on other points in his previous testimony. Then he got to the eyelet and made Kane tell once more where he had found it, after which:

Q—Did you ask him anything about that when you arrested him?

A—No, sir.

Q—You didn't say anything to him about that?

A—No, sir.

Q—There is nothing in the confession about that either, is there?

A—No, sir.

Q—You didn't say anything to Mr. Gibbs when you were questioning him here on this 2½ pages of individual questioning and this long question, as to how he could explain, if at all, if there was any disarrangement or lost eyelet, or anything, in the garter belt?

A—No, sir.

Q—You said nothing to him about that at all?

A—No, sir.

*

Q—Did you make any accusations against him as to any sex impulse on his part?

A—No, sir.

Q—You didn't?

A—No, sir.

Brown held Kane only a few moments more, fixing the location on Marian Baker's wrist of her watch. Ranck came back and questioned Kane as to measurements he had made and approximate driving-time from Lancaster to the site of the murder. Detective Frank P. Matt was called to the stand. Matt, at that time, had been a member of the Lancaster city force for nearly twenty years. He was regarded as a reliable, if not especially brilliant, police officer. He told how he and Corporal Kane had taken Gibbs into custody and how they then took him to Maple Grove so he could demonstrate how he had disposed of Marian Baker's personal effects. From the stand, Matt said:

. . . After he had described these places at the creek, he was taken back to the car. Of course, I got in the back seat with him, and he started to talk again. He then talked about his college education, and he said, "I doubt very much whether you fellows would ever have been able to find out what I did with her personal effects or who did it." He said he felt pretty good when the thing went on for a couple of days, and he thought he might get away with this, but he had watched Kane and I on the campus, and he said when he was sent, called to Dean Breidenstine's office, and Dean Breidenstine gave him the silly excuse about arguing with the professor, he said he knew the police knew more than what they were letting on. He told about watching Kane and I talking to Mr. Crudden, Mr. Barr, and later talking to a man he called his Uncle Tom, who was Tom Floyd, an employee at the college. He said he watched Tom Floyd pointing to the cellar and he thought Tom Floyd might have saw him with the shovel. He then saw Tom Floyd point to his car and later watched Kane and I walk over to his car and look it over. He said it was then he decided to give himself up . . .

Detective Matt volunteered other information that had not been included in Gibbs' signed confession. He said:

I questioned him about this day [*the day of the murder—RG*], about his activities, and he talked about going to this movie with his boy friend and this picture that was supposed to have been shown at the Hamilton Theatre and being pulled out, he thought, due to the fact that there were two strip-tease artists in this picture, Dr. Spotts, a member of the faculty, had ordered the picture out because he is supposed to have censored pictures college boys

168

see on the town. He told about his alibi, that he had told his boy friend that he was going to the Grand Theatre. He said he walked down to the Grand Theatre but didn't go in, stood around and waited a short time, and he saw Marian Baker on North Queen Street. . . .

*

I questioned him about what happened after they pulled up near the Harnish Cottage. . . . He said he had this impulse to choke her, and I asked why, and he said, "I don't know." He said, "She was hard to kill. She didn't want to die," and he told about a brief struggle in the car, about Marian Baker jumping out of the car, and he said she didn't get very far, he was right in back of her, and he grabbed her and choked her, and then went and got the lug wrench, got the ignition keys out of the car, opened the trunk, and got the lug wrench, and then his mind is a blank. He said, "I don't know what happened." That is the general substance of what he said, other than he kept insisting he thought he might have gotten away with this, and he talked about several other murders that were unsolved in the State.

Q—Did he state any reason why he killed her? Did he mention the subject? Did he rule out any possibility?

A—He said it wasn't sex; it wasn't rape. . . . He volunteered that information. Then I questioned him. I said, "Well, when you were hitting her over the head did you get any thrill?

169

Did you notice anything?" He said, "I don't remember." He said, "I can't say what I did, whether it did or didn't." I asked what he did with his underwear, asked him if he noticed anything in his underwear, and he said, "I don't know whether I did or didn't." He said, "I can't remember."

Brown took over. He attacked Detective Matt more relentlessly than he had worked over Corporal Kane, demanding to know why the statement that she didn't want to die had not been included in the confession. Matt said it had not been included because he had not done the questioning when the statement was made. Brown gave the jury a significant glance and caused Matt to reiterate that Gibbs had said that he and Marian Baker had had no conversation in the automobile going down to the cottage. Brown then asked if Gibbs had not made the remark that the tires sounded good, and Matt affirmed that he had. Matt said, "He didn't know whether he said that to Marian Baker or not."

Brown snapped, "Who would he have been saying that to? Was there anybody else in the car?"

Ranck stood up and objected, demanding to know the purpose of the line of questioning. Brown was permitted to continue, and Ranck renewed his objection. Brown's sole purpose here again was to establish some doubt in the jury's minds. He felt that he had accomplished this.

Edgar Rankin was called, sworn, and sent away. Ranck had introduced him to prove, first, that the ring was indeed Marian Baker's, and second, that Rankin and the girl had gone together for two years. Brown objected to this as having no relevancy and as tending to inflame the emotions of the jury. The offer was disallowed, and the witness was withdrawn.

Next, Harry A. Van Bocklin was sworn. He testified that he was a student at Franklin and Marshall College, and that around seven or eight P.M. on the night of January tenth Gibbs had come to his house to pick up a paper which Mrs. Van Bocklin had typed. Van Bocklin said he had left the paper at school. He and Gibbs went upstairs to look at Van Bocklin's baby boy. Van Bocklin said, "I asked him about the scratch on his face and he said it was from basketball."

Brown asked that this testimony be stricken from the record and disregarded by the jury. He was overruled. Now Ranck offered to call two witnesses to whom he knew Brown would object. After a sidebar conference, the counsel, the Judge and the court stenographer retired to Chambers, and the jury was recessed. In Chambers, Ranck named his two witnesses. He said he would call George Marvell, son of an undertaker, who had occupied the apartment next to Gibbs in East Hall, and who would testify that Gibbs had asked him several questions about the decomposition of dead bodies. Marvell would also testify that Gibbs had told him that he had picked up Marian Baker and driven her to the city on the day she was murdered. Brown objected strenuously to bringing Marvell into the case; he said the witness would have nothing to do with proving the offense. The Court sustained his objection, stating that it was so doing because the defendant had not objected to having his confession admitted. Then Ranck, without much optimism, asked to call Kenneth Willig, another undertaker's son, who would testify that Gibbs had asked him substantially the same questions as he had asked Marvell. Brown again objected and was sustained. The conference continued:

MR. RANCK: The Commonwealth offers to call as a witness Sgt. Strickler, Pennsylvania State Police, Crime Detection Laboratory, Harrisburg, who will testify he has made microscopic examinations of the eyelet which was found near the scene of the murder with the eyelet on the garter belt which has been identified as "Q.S. No. 61" and will state that they are identical in appearance.

MR. BROWN: Objected to, if the Court please, to the expert witness testifying to the fact that the eyelet allegedly found by Corporal Kane at the scene or 12 feet from the scene on the ground, not that he isn't qualified to testify from chemical or laboratory tests, it appears to be an identical eyelet of the type in Exhibit "Q.S. No. 61," but on the ground that "Q.S. No. 61" should not have been admitted into evidence because there was no evidence the defendant tore this eyelet from the garter belt.

THE COURT: Objection overruled.

MR. RANCK: Now, if the Court please, we offer to call Gordon K. Hausrath and Richard Graybill, who will testify that in the fall of 1949 they were on a paint detail at F. & M. College with the defendant, Edward Gibbs, that while they were working Marian Baker walked by the defendant, Edward L. Gibbs, stated in their hearing, "I would like to make her." If the Court please, from every indication thus far in this case, from the confession of Gibbs, both orally and in writing, there has been a studied effort to remove any sexual implication from this crime. We are offering this evidence to show

172

the state of mind of the defendant with reference to this particular girl, or woman, he later admitted killing. We also introduce it as testimony bearing on the motive for the killing.

MR. BROWN: We object strenuously to that as extremely remote, 6 or 8 months removed from the time of the crime, that it is not a relevant part of the Commonwealth's case, and is irrelevant, immaterial and incompetent.

THE COURT: Objection sustained.

The gentlemen returned to the Courtroom, and the jury was brought back. John J. Coll, a State Police officer, was questioned on Gibbs' flashlight, which he had obtained from the home of Gibbs' father-in-law. It was admitted as evidence. Sgt. Peter Strickler, chemist with the Pennsylvania State Police, was called and testified that the eyelet found at the scene was identical with those on Marian Baker's garter belt. Brown attempted to challenge his testimony by pointing out that the eyelets could have been used in "hundreds of thousands of similar garments." He moved that the testimony be stricken from the record, and was overruled. Sgt. Vernon E. Simpson was sworn. He testified to finding the blood spot on the Harnish property and corroborated the testimony of Matt and Kane. The District Attorney said, "I wish to make a blanket offer in evidence of all exhibits which I may have inadvertently not offered in evidence and which the Court has not already ruled out."

"They are admitted," said Judge Wissler.

"The Commonwealth rests," said Ranck.

Brown, without any hope, purely as an automatic legal gesture, filed a demurrer to the evidence. A demurrer is a plea which, while admitting the truth of the opposite party's case, contends that it is insufficient in law to uphold his claim, or that there is some other legal reason why the opposing party should not be allowed to continue the case. The demurrer said:

> . . . the said Edward Lester Gibbs, defendant, in his own proper person comes into Court and having heard the Evidence produced by the Commonwealth says that the said evidence and matters therein are as therein alleged and set forth and proven, insufficient in law to warrant a conviction of the defendant of either murder in the first or second degree and this he, the said Edward Lester Gibbs, is ready to verify. Therefore, he prays judgment and asks that by the Court here he may be dismissed and discharged from the charges of murder in the first and second degree as set forth in the indictment against him.

The demurrer was overruled.

Brown next moved that the Court direct a verdict of not guilty of murder in the first degree, or murder in the second degree, or voluntary manslaughter. This too was overruled. The Court was adjourned for lunch.

Brown's opening speech was as terse as Ranck's had been. He said, "Ladies and gentlemen of the jury, as stated by Mr. Ranck, this is a serious case. It is serious to the Commonwealth and serious to the defendant. In those remarks, I heartily concur. However, there are a great deal of disputed facts. You have heard admitted into evidence Mr. Gibbs' confession. You have heard the Commonwealth's testimony . . ." From there, Brown outlined the testimony he would present. He concluded by stating that he would not argue what the verdict should be; he said,

"I prefer you should hear the testimony of Mr. Gibbs and other witnesses first, and then I will recommend a verdict in my humble opinion."

Gibbs was called to the stand as Brown's first move. He wore the same light brown suit as he had worn the day before, but the figured necktie had been replaced by a solid brown one. He was escorted to the stand by Elmer Zerphey, a Deputy Sheriff. He did not seem nervous; all observers, in fact, were impressed by his calm—by his cold-bloodedness, as some termed it. He answered all questions in a quiet, respectful voice, as though he were being interviewed for a job. The reporters later said that his only sign of tension was a continual licking of his lips, as though his mouth were becoming dry from having talked so long. His father, still sitting with Reverend Guice, seemed more affected by the ordeal of testimony.

Brown kept Gibbs on the stand approximately thirty-five minutes. The young man laid his entire early life before the court. He told about his home town, his school days, his Army career, his entry into college, and his marriage. He verbally re-enacted the events of the day of the murder, beginning with his trip to the movies with John George. He told of meeting Marian Baker. He held himself well under control. Brown questioning:

Q—Did you know her before?
A—Yes, sir, I knew her around college.
Q—How well did you know her?
A—Just enough to say hello to. Just as well as I knew the other secretaries out there. She cashed my checks. I would stop at the office and say hello when I was cashing checks or anything like that, but nothing anything more than

casually, than you would know any other secretary on the campus when you have been there the time I have.

Gibbs, still speaking calmly, went over the brief conversation he had had with Marian Baker, and told how they had got in his car and driven south on Prince Street. He insisted that she had done all the talking; he said:

> . . . she was talking about college, graduation, caps and gowns, year books, just college talk in general, which was our only common, what we had in common to talk about . . .

Gibbs described the remainder of the drive and went on to the point where he had stopped the car. Brown asked him what happened then. Gibbs' answer, and the subsequent interrogation:

> A—We sat there for, I don't know, it wasn't a very long time, and something just happened inside of me, I don't know, I don't know what happened, I can't explain it, but I just reached over and grabbed her and started to choke her.
>
> Q—She was sitting to your right?
>
> A—That is right, sir. She screamed and got out of the car and I chased her and I grabbed her, and this part of it I am not absolutely certain about. I know what must have happened, because I can see, after I remember it, after I came to myself again I can remember how it was, but I am not absolutely positive of it. The next thing I actually remember is looking

176

down and seeing blood on my hands and the lug wrench along side of me.

Q—The last thing you remember is her getting out of the car?

A—Her getting out of the car and catching up with her.

*

Q—Then what did you do?

A—After seeing what happened, I saw this pump and I went over and took the wire off and tried to pump it to wash the blood off my hands. Unable to get water out I left and went back and my first impulse was to go to the police and tell them what had happened, but self-preservation is a big instinct in any person, and then I decided it would be best if I didn't do this, and I, I started to, I tried to pick the body up. I got her up but she was too heavy, I couldn't handle her. I laid her down again and then started to drag her by the hands, but this didn't work out too successfully.

Q—Which way did you drag her?

A—Down over the middle of the hill. Then I grabbed her by the feet and started dragging her down and I drug her down over the middle of the hill, down by the garbage piles, to the place I indicated to Officer Kane I had first put the body. . . . Then I left. I took the lug wrench and my clothes and went back to the college by a very roundabout route, as I had blood all over my hands, all over my face, on my jacket. It had trickled over on my pants and socks and sleeveless sweater . . .

He went on, adding minor details to the information already brought out and admitted, describing his movements after he returned to the scene. Brown asked him what he had done after his return, and he said he had picked up his wife at Armstrong Cork. They had gone to dinner with H. W. Leary and his wife. Gibbs then described his unsuccessful attempt to bury the body, his visit to Van Bocklin's house, and his concealment of the body under the corrugated sheet. Finally Brown said:

Q—At any time when you stopped the car, did you assault Miss Baker, attempt to have intercourse with her?

A—No, sir.

Q—Did you tell Officer Matt you had made up your mind to do something to her while driving down the highway that day?

A—No, I did not.

Q—Did you intend to do any harm to her at all that day?

A—No, sir, I did not.

*

Q—Now, did you tell Officer Matt or Officer Kane that she was hard to kill and she didn't want to die?

A—No, sir, I did not.

Q—Did you say you were a college man and sorry you did it?

A—Yes, sir, I did.

Q—You didn't say the other?

A—No, sir.

Brown next questioned Gibbs about his financial condition prior to the murder. Gibbs said that he and his wife owed approximately $400. He owed $70 to Franklin and Marshall, he said, $30 to the school bookshop, $55.75 on his automobile, $25.00 to the Fraternity, and $20 in monthly installments to the Household Finance Company. He did not say how large a loan he and his wife had made from the company; he said that none of the bills were "pressing." Satisfied that Gibbs had made a favorable impression with his quiet, respectful answers, Brown relinquished him for cross-examination. Ranck began slowly. He first established the fact that Gibbs believed the confession correct as he had written it, and that it had been entirely voluntary. Then the District Attorney worked around to the point he had been trying to make throughout the trial.

> Q— . . . on the day on question, January 10 . . . you saw an advertisement for the movie at the Hamilton and you and John George decided to go to it; is that correct?
>
> A—That is right, sir.
>
> Q—When you got to the Hamilton Theatre you found, as you described it, the picture had been pulled?
>
> A—Yes, sir.

*

> Q—Now, I ask you, Ed, what was the name of the picture you intended to see?
>
> A—I had no idea, sir. There were two of them, and I had no idea.

*

> Q—Whether you remember the name of the pictures, do you remember the principal actresses who were in the pictures? Now, this is the one that was advertised that you went to see.

179

A—No, sir, I do not. The only thing I remember about them, that they had been former burlesque girls.

Q—Do you remember saying something to the officers about your intention to see a sexy movie?

A—I remember saying what I was going downtown to see, the movie, but I don't remember whether I said it was a sexy movie, or not.

Q—Do you remember any mention of burlesque queens made by you to anyone?

A—It could have been; I don't recall.

Q—If I tell you the movie advertised for that day starred Ann Corio and Margie Hart was starred in the other, would that refresh your recollection?

A—That could have been the names, sir.

Q—What do you know about those two stars?

A—I only know they are burlesque girls.

Q—They are well-known burlesque girls?

A—Yes, sir.

Ranck then had Gibbs admit that it was two P.M. when he decided not to go to the movies because the bill had been taken off. Gibbs said that he could have gone back to the college to study until five, when he was to go to pick up his wife. Then Ranck directed his attention to the meeting with Marian Baker:

Q—Had you ever had Marian in your car before under any circumstances?

A—Not to my knowledge, sir. She may have been in there going down or coming back.

Not to my actual knowledge, because I drove back and forth from college quite a bit and took quite a few people back and forth, and it was possible she was in the car.

Q—Do I understand that frequently, on other occasions, you drove girls back and forth to the college?

A—Not girls, fellows and girls.

Q—But you also drove girls?

A—Yes, sir.

Q— . . . you are not sure whether she was in the car before, but she may have been?

A—She could have been.

Q—Could it have been possible that she was ever in your car alone, before? I mean, just you and Marian. Could that be possible?

A—Yes, that could be possible.

With the confession in his hand, Ranck began methodically verifying Gibbs' statements as to how he had killed the girl, in what position her body had been, and how far he had dragged it. He posed his questions with a scientific precision, trying to make certain damning points, among which were these:

Q—Isn't it a fact you told the Police you dragged her solely by the legs?

A—No, sir.

*

Q—She was face down and you drug her by the hands?

A—Yes, sir.

Q—You heard the testimony about the garter belt in Court today?

A—Yes, sir.

Q—You heard the officer testify the eyelet was found about 12 feet from the blood spot where you killed Marian?

A—Yes, sir.

Q—Does that have any significance in your statement that you dragged her by the arms about 11 feet?

A—No, sir.

*

Q—Did you hear the Doctor, Dr. Heid, and the Officers testify that . . . there were no rips or tears in the stockings?

A—Yes, sir.

Q—Will you describe . . . if you can, the area . . . through which you dragged the body?

A—It is just ground with leaves over it.

Q—There were also pebbles around there?

A—I don't recall, sir.

Q— . . . You want us to understand you dragged this girl by the arms, on her face, and it didn't tear her stockings?

A—Sir, I lifted her up as much as I could by dragging.

Q—What parts of the body would have been touching?

A—Her toes and thighs, and this part of her. I guess they call that the thighs.

Q—If you wanted to drag her down to the garbage pile, why did you not continue to drag her by the hands, if you started in that fashion?

A—Because it was too hard, sir.

*

Q—Now, Edward, you testified when you were in high school you were active in athletics?

A—That is right, sir . . . I won 4 varsity letters in different sports.

*

Q—Did you win any of those letters after the accident you described?

A—Yes, sir, all of them after this accident.

Q—Did that blow on the head physically handicap you in any way?

A—Not to my knowledge, sir.

Q— . . . How did you do with your school work in high school?

A—Not too well, but good enough to get by.

Q— . . . When you entered the service you went into pilot training as a cadet; is that correct?

A—That is right, sir.

Q—Now, as I understand it, Eddie, in the army, unlike some other branches of the service, if a man trying out for pilot failed, there was certain other alternatives he could try and still remain.

*

A—At the time I went through you either made pilot training—you were classed either as a pilot, a bombardier, or a navigator. You were given no second choice of another position because the war was well under way and there was a back-lash. We were all waiting around to move to the next phase, and they didn't have to take time on anybody they weren't sure wasn't going to make the grade.

MR. BROWN: Back-lash or log?

THE WITNESS: Log.

Q—When you washed out as a pilot my question is simply this: Were all doors to becoming an officer closed to you at that time?

A—They were, sir.

Q—What next did you try?

A—I went into a radio school as a code man to work in nets.

*

Q—You washed out of that, too?

A—Yes, sir.

Q—Isn't it a fact, Eddie, that thousands of boys had the identical experience you did?

A—Yes, sir.

Q—A great many boys who had pilot training washed out, didn't they?

A—Yes, sir.

Q—And a great number that tried that radio training washed out?

A—Yes, sir.

Q—Is it a tough course unless you have a mind attuned to code?

A—That is right.

Q—Then to get it pretty fast you have to learn to read it quickly?

A—No, sir I first learned at that time at Scott Field.

Q—You had difficulty with it?

A—The constant drilling of that code into my ears and into my head, I couldn't stand it.

Q—You were not in combat, were you?

A—No sir. . . .

*

Q—You were not subjected to any bombing?

A—We had anti-aircraft guns around the field but as long as I was there we were never under any bombardment . . .

Q—Never attacked?

A—That is right.

Q—You testified that while at that field you had certain harrowing occurrences, you had crashes and you had gasoline go up, and you had planes come in with landing gear stuck, perilous landings, and things of that nature; is that right?

A—That is right.

Q—Doesn't that happen at every field?

A—Yes, it does, sir.

Q—There was nothing particularly unusual about your field?

A—Only that we had Italians flying off the field over which we had no control whatsoever; they did as they pleased.

Q—Although you controlled our planes, you didn't know when they were going to come in and louse up the deal; is that right?

A—That is right.

Q—Now, Ed, you testified you were flunking psychology and Spanish?

A—That is right.

Q—Weren't you flunking anything else?

A—I felt I was flunking corporation finance, but I wasn't sure.

Q—Then it was still humanly possible you could have graduated?

A—But I also had to have everything in my last, every Senior subject . . . to graduate —a flunk in any course would have caused me not to graduate.

Q— . . . In view of this statement of yours that you . . . were terribly worried about flunking, and you state your mother was horribly upset about your flunking, can you explain why you were going to the movies on the 10th of January?

A—Exams were coming next week and I was simply trying to relax my mind, some diversion. You can study just so long before things start to go around.

Q—How about all those other movies downtown? You had seen all those?

A—Yes, I had.

Q—Were you getting diversion at that time, too?

A—Yes, sir.

Q—When did you see the other movies, in the evening with your wife, or in the afternoon?

A—Both, sir.

*

Q—For mental relaxation you wanted to go see Ann Corio and Margie Hart?

A—I wanted to see a movie, sir.

Q—Let's get this straight. You have testified that this is the movie you wanted to see?

A—That is the one they were showing, yes, sir.

Q—Now, Edward, I think you testified, as I mentioned before, you had difficulty making arrangements at the movie that particular afternoon, January 10th, and you decided to go back and work. Now what made you change your mind when you saw Marian Baker?

A—I was still seeking—you mean why we went for the drive?

Q—Why did you change your mind about going back to work?

A—I was seeking relaxation.

Q—Your thought was then not to merely render taxi service so that you could get to work?

A—Up until we stopped at the red light, yes, sir.

Q—What made you change your mind when you got to the red light?

A—I don't know, sir.

Q—Did you have any irresistible impulse to do anything at that time?

A—No, sir.

*

Q—She was an attractive person?

A—At times I have seen her when she has been very attractive; at other times I have seen her not so attractive. She was a nice looking girl.

Q—How was she this day?

A—She made no striking impression on me.

*

187

Q—Now, Edward, will you please tell the Court and Jury what was the weather like that afternoon?

A—As I recall it, it was a dull day.

*

Q—It wasn't a clear, sparkling day like it is today?

A—No, sir.

Q—Yet you wanted to go for a drive?

A—I was seeking relaxation, sir.

Q—Seeking relaxation from what?

A—From the pent-up feeling that exams were coming, I wasn't going to pass, I wanted something to relax my mind so I could study.

Still proceeding with what must have been, to Gibbs, painful methodism, Ranck made him go over the details of the ride again and again. He kept trying to make Gibbs say that he had said something more than the remark about the tires singing on the bridge, and Gibbs kept strictly to the story as he had told it so many times before. Ranck then proceeded to the actual act of murder:

Q—And how long from the moment you stopped, how much time intervened until you had your hands on her throat?

A—I don't know, but the interval could not have been very long.

*

Q—How long did you choke her in the car?

A—I don't know, sir.

Q—Well, do you think you did it one minute, or 2 minutes, or what?

A—It wasn't a very long time because she

screamed and got immediately out of the car.

Q—Where had you touched her up to that point?

A—I hadn't touched her until I reached for her throat.

Q—Are you sure you didn't reach any place else?

A—No, sir.

*

Q—Where did you put your hands on her throat, which hand on which portion of her neck?

A—I don't know, sir.

*

Q—Did she remonstrate, did she say anything, "Eddie, what are you doing? Are you out of your mind?" Anything of that nature?

A—Not that I recall.

Q—You heard her scream?

A—Yes, sir.

*

Q—At any rate, she jumped out, and how far did she get before you touched her again?

A—I don't know.

Q—Well, 5 feet, 10 feet, 20 feet?

A—I have no idea.

Ranck produced "Q. S. No. 5," showing the position the body was found in under the Harnish Cottage. Gibbs said he had never seen the photograph before. Ranck went on:

Q—Do you notice the position of the coat on her body?

*

A—It seems to be off her shoulders.

Q— . . . Can you explain why it would be off her shoulders?

A—No, sir, I cannot.

*

Q—Would it be possible that you grabbed her by the back of the coat and pulled it down, pinning her arms? Would that be possible?

A—It could be, but I don't recall.

Q—Would you, by any chance—I don't know whether you testified to this or Mr. Brown stated it—have tackled her?

A—I said later on it would be entirely possible I could have tackled her. From playing football it would seem like a natural instinct, if I wanted to bring somebody to the ground.

Q—Did your impulse continue after you got out of the car?

A—This part I don't know, entirely remember.

Q—But you did remember it at one time, didn't you?

A—In my statement I told them how it must have happened from my recollection of what I discovered . . .

Q—But you didn't say that in your statement?

A—No, sir, I didn't.

Q—You gave them a recount of what had happened as you remembered it, is that correct?

A—Yes, sir, that is right.

Q—And several days elapsed between the

time you killed this girl and made this statement?

A—Yes, sir, they had.

Q—You had a lot of time to think this over?

A—Yes, I had.

Q—Several days before you confessed you could feel the dragnet closing in on you?

A—Not several days.

Q—When?

A—The day I confessed, that afternoon after returning from downtown.

Q—Didn't you make a statement you were worried when they didn't question you that week?

A—I might have said I thought I should have been questioned because they were questioning anybody with a car.

Q—You weren't thinking of much else from the time you killed her until you confessed?

A—No, sir.

*

Q—And you want us to understand that you did this on impulse?

A—That is right, sir.

Q—How much was impulse, and how much deliberate?

A—All of it was impulse, sir.

*

Q—When did the impulse stop? After you got out of the car and wholly choked her?

A—I don't recall anything until I came to and saw the blood on my hands and the lug wrench.

*

Q—Edward, wouldn't you feel better if you told us all exactly what happened down there that day?

A—I have told you exactly what happened.

*

Q—. . . Isn't it possible that you might have forgotten that you grabbed her by the garter belt?

A—I don't recall ever trying to grab her by the garter belt.

Q—Isn't it possible you might have but you have forgotten about it?

A—No, sir.

*

Q—Could you be positive you didn't touch her?

A—No, sir.

*

Q—Now, Edward, did you, on any occasion prior to January 10th, 1950, state to anyone you would like to make Marian Baker?

Brown jumped to his feet, objected, and was sustained. The Court instructed the Jury to disregard the statement. Sidebar, Ranck then proposed to ask the defendant questions concerning a girl he allegedly had taken out on a date in 1949 (*the M.E.C.—referred to previously —RG*). Brown was also sustained in his objection to this. After a few more questions having to do with the place Gibbs had bought his flashlight, and after asking Gibbs to identify the lug wrench and the shovel, Ranck gave him up. Reporters later called his interrogation "the most vigorous cross-examination given in recent years in the Lancaster County courts." Ranck had kept Gibbs on the stand eighty minutes. Still, Brown was not discouraged. He felt that Gibbs had done well.

The next witness was the one on whom Brown was counting most. He was Dr. Edward A. Strecker, the psychiatrist. A gray-haired, professorial individual with the ring of authority in his voice, Dr. Strecker is a veteran of countless trials involving persons whose legal sanity is questioned. His background and record are impeccable. He graduated from Jefferson Medical College in Philadelphia in 1911. At the time he testified in Gibbs' behalf, he was Professor of Psychology and Chairman of the Department of Psychology, Under Graduate School of Medicine, University of Pennsylvania, and Professor of Psychology in the Graduate School; consultant in Psychiatry for the Secretary of War to the Surgeon General, a Naval consultant, and a consultant to the U.S. Public Health Service and the Veterans Administration. Dr. Strecker had examined Gibbs twice in the Lancaster County Prison, on February first and February twenty-eighth, and in addition he had initiated several other examinations, including a neurological examination, an X-ray examination of the skull, an electroencephalographic examination, and a Rorschach test. He first reviewed his qualifications under Brown's questioning, and then went briefly into Gibbs' family background and experiences as he saw them (all of this has been outlined or quoted in the preceding chapter). He said, at one point, "There were a number of indications in the history which tend to show there were times when he quite lost control of his behavior." He mentioned a letter from Dr. Friedlin reporting on the incident when Gibbs had so dramatically lost his temper at dinner, and he mentioned the psychologist's report made at Franklin and Marshall. Then he said:

> . . . I would like to now give briefly the results of the . . . various examinations beginning with those that revealed the least information, but still some. The neurological examination showed no evidence of any gross disease of the central nervous system. The electroencephalographic study [is] . . . a method of attempting to determine gross disease or abnormality of the brain by studying the graph which is produced by the machine—that was made in Philadelphia. Its chief purpose is to help in the diagnosis of epilepsy. It also, however, reveals sometimes other diseases and abnormalities of the brain. It was in this instance negative . . . That has a negative value. It, however, does not have a complete value because even in true epilepsy approximately 15% of the electroencephalograms are negative. It has some value, and I certainly should not want to make a diagnosis of epilepsy. However, also, I certainly should not want to say that this young man's brain and personality was not possibly damaged to some extent by his first cerebral concussion. I couldn't be sure. I think it is some-

thing that has to be taken into consideration to get a true and valid picture. . . . Now, the X-ray of the skull . . . was certainly, for the purposes of this case, negative. There was a spur of bone on one side which I could not possibly say would have any relationship to the problem we are trying to solve. It may have had some influence on the sinus condition which this young man has . . . but I would regard it as rather incidental. . . . I will speak on my own examination next, a true psychiatric examination, and I will say it did not show any marked out-spoken symptoms of actual mental disease or insanity. On the other hand, I could not, by any matter of means, regard Edward Gibbs as normal mentally since there was so much evidence against it . . . the examination confirmed the evidence of the history and of my conversations with him that he was extremely immature, very insecure, and very inadequate in his personality. Furthermore, I felt it revealed that his emotional reactions were not often in keeping, not strong enough for the content of thought. Psychiatrists speak of this as disassociation. They sometimes call it schizophrenia, which means some splitting, some disproportion between the emotional reactions as expressed by the patient and the content of his thought. . . . On the basis of that, partly, and because I feel it is . . . important . . . I asked permission and was granted permission to have a so-called Rorschach examination made, and this was done at the Lancaster County prison on February 8. . . . The test was made and

195

recorded by Miss Eleanor Ross, who is a psychiatrist and a qualified diplomate of the American Rorschach Institute . . . I felt this examination very important because there were no definite and serious out-spoken symptoms of mental disease but enough there to make one feel . . . I will satisfy myself and you by saying that she made a diagnosis of schizophrenia . . . I regard the Rorschach test as very scientific, well-tried, in common use in all good mental hospitals, relied on by the majority of psychiatrists I know, and in my opinion the interpretation has been in agreement with my own opinion and diagnosis in more than 95% of the cases.

*

Q—Now, will you give us the results?

A—The . . . examination . . . led her to make the diagnosis of schizophrenia.

*

Q—In other words, it corresponded very largely, if not entirely, with your own diagnostic results?

A—I want to make clear again: I did not find marked and out-spoken symptoms of mental disease in my examination. I did find enough to make me consider very seriously whether there was not an underlying psychosis.

Q—Will you give us your diagnosis again?

A—. . . while I do not believe Eddie Gibbs was totally irresponsible, or completely incapable of distinguishing between right and wrong, yet I believe very strongly and very definitely his degree of responsibility, both medical and legal, must be assessed at very much less than that of the normal person, and that in both the psychiatric and legal sense he has an abnormal personality, and at the time of the crime and at this time has a latent psychosis, or mental disease, schizophrenia. . . . Therefore I [say] his responsibility must be assessed at much less than the average person. . . . I therefore believe he did not have sufficient or average capacity to understand the nature and quality of his act.

Q—In the normal course of his studies, daily occupations . . . would he appear certainly normal most times?

A—Yes, I think that makes no difference. For instance, the Veteran's Bureau psychiatrists have many patients who are schizophrenic under out-patient treatment. The doctors know they have schizophrenia and may blow up at some time, but they continue, very often, with some form of daily occupation.

Q—How is a schizophrenic affected by memory of details?

A—I know of nothing in schizophrenia which particularly affects the memory, though it may appear so because in advanced stages of illness the patient gives the picture of such indifference to the outer world that it would appear he doesn't remember, but it has been demonstrated time and time again that his memory can come back and he can be very clear in his remembrance.

Q—Would it make any difference in your opinion, Doctor, that the examination you conducted, as well as the ones made under your direction, were made approximately a month after the offense was committed?

*

A—Not in my opinion.

Q—You feel the same results would have been obtained had the examination been made on January 10th, 1950?

A—Yes, sir.

Ranck took over the witness. He leaped immediately to the attack, catching up Dr. Strecker on his previous answer.

Q—What time, January 10th, 1950?

A—You mean what time of the day?

Q—That is right.

A—Well, I don't know that I quite get the purpose of your question. I was going to add the same result would have been obtained if made sometime before. I don't know—

Q—That is what I want to establish. Mr. Brown said would it make any difference if made on January 10, 1950. It has been testified . . . this defendant killed Marian Baker on that date . . . I would like you to answer the question whether it would make any difference if the examination was given before or after that hour on January 10th, 1950?

A—Whether the examination had been made just before the crime . . . was committed, or immediately after?

MR. BROWN: Or the day before, or the day after.

THE WITNESS: I believe the same results would have been obtained.

MR. RANCK: Are you positive of that?

A—I am as positive as one can be in testifying about something that is an art and not an exact science, psychiatry.

Q—We all admit it is not an exact science.

A—And the law, too.

Q—We can try to pierce through some of the words that have been used.

A—I am sorry if I used any too technical. I particularly tried not to.

Q—I believe I understand some of them. I don't know whether the jury understands them all. My question I am now directing to you is this: Are you familiar with the legal test of insanity?

A—Yes, indeed.

Q—Will you describe it to the jury?

A—I have to ask for a little leeway, because frankly I think the legal attitude about insanity is now in the process of change. I don't think it is governed now in the main by your McNaughton case.

Q—I am not asking your predictions as to what it is going to be.

A—I am not predicting. I base that on my own experience.

Both Ranck and Storb later told friends that the witness was the most elusive, shifting, evasive they had ever questioned. Now Ranck turned to the bench in controlled exasperation. "If the Court please, as I see this, his answer is not responsive to my question."

Brown stood up. "He said he is familiar with the legal definition."

Judge Wissler said, "The question asked, if I recall it, is whether he is familiar with the legal definition of insanity."

Dr. Strecker turned toward the Judge. "I am, Your Honor, and strictly speaking, legally, it is still based on the McNaughton case, 115 years ago."

Ranck resumed his questioning:

Q—Just describe it.

A—Well, the McNaughton case, as it becomes codified, strictly speaking, legally raises the question of the capacity to distinguish between right and wrong. I don't know that it was well qualified even in the McNaughton case.

Q—Would this meet your understanding of it? It is the ability of one to distinguish right from wrong, to appreciate the consequences of one's act, and also to appreciate the value and quality of the act when he did it?

A—I think that would cover what was laid down in the McNaughton case.

Q—Wouldn't that also cover what is the present law in Pennsylvania today, from your knowledge?

A—That is the law. I think I should be permitted to say in my experience as an expert I have noticed a very definite change in the attitude of the Courts about the interpretation of the McNaughton case.

Brown rose to bolster his witness. "For instance, Doctor?"

Ranck would not permit the witness to offer an example. "I am objecting again," he said. "I asked whether he knows the rule in Pennsylvania. I am not asking him to prognosticate what is going to happen in the future."

The Judge nodded. "Yes, we are confined to the law as it now is."

Ranck continued:

> Q—According to the law . . . is this man responsible for his act?

*

> A—I don't think that is fair. I testified and so say—I said he had some capacity to distinguish between right and wrong. I also said I didn't consider he had the capacity to understand the quality and nature of his act.

The District Attorney clung to his point relentlessly. He demanded again to know if Gibbs was legally sane, under the law, at the time he committed his act. Dr. Strecker:

> . . . He was legally sane under the strict interpretation of the McNaughton rule. I do not know whether I could say that as to the exact minute the murder was committed.

Now Ranck switched his attack. He asked if Dr. Strecker had found that latent schizophrenia existed in Gibbs when he had examined him on February 1. The Doctor said that he had not had enough evidence to make a definite clinical diagnosis. He added, under questioning, that he also had not had enough evidence after February 28. Ranck went on:

> Q—What transpired subsequent to February 28 . . . that would cause you to move forward to your present diagnosis?
>
> A—First, my own feeling, which was formed and which was pretty strong, and then the support of the Rorschach test.
>
> Q—Now, Doctor, let me ask you this. . . . Would you, as an expert in the field of psychiatry, which we all admit is not an exact science, reach a conclusion or diagnosis of latent schizophrenia based solely on the Rorschach test?
>
> A—Not solely, but he didn't pass the Rorschach test.
>
> Q—I said would you, solely under the Rorschach test, come to that conclusion?
>
> A—It would depend—

Ranck addressed the bench once more. "That is not responsive."

"Let the Doctor finish," said the Judge.

Dr. Strecker said, "I was only going to say it would depend on the individual case."

Ranck asked the Stenographer to read the question again. Strecker:

> . . . I don't think so. I am not trying to be difficult. I am saying you are imposing an impossible situation. You are imposing a situation in which from my examination I would have no opinion either way, and that is not possible.

202

Q—You are saying, as I understand it, from a practical viewpoint you wouldn't do it that way?

A—You mean if I didn't see the patient at all, would I make a diagnosis on Rorschach alone, but you can't ask me to say after examining a patient I come out of that examination without any feeling or opinion at all.

Q—That wasn't quite what I asked you, Doctor.

A—Well—

Ranck again dropped the issue and went on to other parts of the Doctor's previous testimony. He asked if it were not a fact that most of the information about Gibbs had come from Gibbs himself. Dr. Strecker replied that much had, but not all; he had obtained some from Brown, some from Dr. Friedlin, and some from Dr. Nelson, who had looked after Gibbs when he was suffering from concussion. Ranck asked if Gibbs' testimony about his sexual relations with his wife were unconfirmed, and the Doctor admitted that it was. Ranck:

Q—Now, Doctor, I understood you to testify . . . you found Edward to be afraid of physical violence?

A—Yes . . . that came from him. . . . He didn't say he evaded all fights; he did sometimes fight, but he told me he was always afraid. That has whatever value his statement may have.

Q—It has been testified . . . he was a four-letter man . . . that he attempted to make the Varsity football team at F & M . . . he went out and rescued this burning truck . . .

does that correspond to a person who is afraid of physical violence?

A—No, sir, but I also have seen many men who are athletes, many men during the war who were brave soldiers, gallant soldiers, had orders for certain things, and who were still afraid of physical violence. They overcame at that particular time that particular facet of their personality.

Q—But were they under orders?

A—Yes, but they could easily get out of it.

Q—Would that apply to a man that goes out for the football team?

A—I will say I have known athletes who . . . had to overcome very strong reactions and fears about physical violence. . . .

Q—Then the only reason you think he was afraid is because Edward told you so?

A—That is the chief reason, yes, sir.

Q—You are not sure he was telling the truth?

A—And my evaluation of the rest of his personality. Persons who are as emotionally immature, insecure as he is, and passive—by passive meaning persons who tend to be emotionally dependent—they are usually somewhat afraid of physical violence, but not necessarily always so.

Q—What, if any, mental symptoms did you find in your clinical examination?

A—I said I found no outspoken mental symptoms. I did find enough to make me feel there was a strong possibility of an underlying psychosis or a very serious personality deviation.

*

Q—He cried when you talked to him?

A—He didn't the first time; he did the second.

Q—You saw him on the stand today?

A—Yes, sir.

Q—You reached the same conclusion from him on the stand today, or not?

A—Not exactly the same. I felt he did not show a very complete emotional reaction to your cross-examination.

Q—Do you think he was telling the truth?

*

A—I don't know. I think he was. I don't know, but I mean he showed comparatively little emotional reaction to your masterly cross-examination.

Q—And yet you testified that while you examined him in the prison . . . he cried?

A—He did, the second time. He was pretty tearful . . . and he was frightened.

*

Q—Did he cry too little or too much, in your opinion, on the second examination?

A—. . . He cried a good deal. The examination wasn't very satisfactory.

Q—. . . for what reason?

A—Because he was crying so much.

*

Q—Didn't that indicate anything to you?
A—He was frightened.

*

Q—Doctor, wouldn't it be perfectly normal and natural for a man indicted for murder to be frightened?
A—Yes, it would. I indicated that at the second examination he showed more emotional reaction. At first it was very inadequate, straying off to inconsequential things. Yet, here was a man facing trial for his life.

*

Q—Did this man have delusions and distortions in connection with reality?
A—No delusions that I was able to discover.
Q—Will you list briefly the cardinal symptoms of a schizophrenic personality?
A—Briefly, it is pretty hard to do. I will try . . . There are many different varieties of schizophrenia . . . as reactions types . . . the symptoms may be so slight that a skilled psychiatrist needs a long time to come to a conclusion. They may be so obvious that any layman may know a person is very sick mentally. There are great varieties of symptoms. There may be paranoic reactions, ideas of suspicion, there may be hallucinations of hearing; there may be simple deterioration; there may be what we call cataleptic stupor . . . there may be symptoms, none of these symptoms marked or even present

206

for any long period of time, but the psychosis may be encompassed in a gradual withdrawal from reality . . .

Q—Which of these symptoms did you find to be present in the defendant?

A—I found chiefly what I thought was inadequacy in his affections, he had the kind of personality, schizophrenic, emotionally immature, dependency, rather afraid of the world.

Q—Aren't they present in a great many people?

A—I hope not too many, because emotional immaturity is a very serious thing.

Q—What do you mean by emotional immaturity?

A—It means a person . . . is not prepared or equipped to meet the personal realities of adult life.

*

Q—. . . if they were present in a particular individual that would be very obvious to his friends?

A—Not necessarily, no. If friends knew him a long time they would speak of him as a person who has no, who is not independently minded, who is emotionally dependent, who is too closely tied to his mother, who has never broken away from his mother. His friends of long standing would discuss him in those terms. It wouldn't stand out.

Q—. . . his college friends . . . would they notice these things you found if he had them to the degree you testified?

A—. . . Some might, some might not. They wouldn't be equal in experience.

Q—I asked you if it were not a fact that many people had these things you mentioned, and you said you hoped not. Why?

A—. . . if we had too many emotionally immature people I think our democracy would be doomed . . .

Q—Can you pick these people out?

A—I can, yes.

Q—You can pick them out of a crowd like this?

A—No. I have got to know about them.

Q—How long?

A—I have to examine them . . .

*

Q—I am asking what showed this boy to have an inadequate personality other than what he has told you?

A—I hope I have some capability and skill as a psychiatrist.

Q—All I am asking is the basis on which you made your diagnosis.

A—Any psychiatrist examining him couldn't come to any other conclusion. I am not talking about schizophrenia, but about emotional immaturity.

*

Q—How many other things would you have to find . . . to classify him as being latent schizophrenic?

208

A—Well, you would have to find such things as symptoms with the support of tests, like the Rorschach. . . . You would have to have a complete examination.

Q—Now I have heard emotional immaturity as one thing you gave for reaching the diagnosis.

A—And emotional inadequacy.

Q—In addition to the Rorschach test, give me some more reasons for reaching your conclusions.

A—I said I found enough . . . to raise a very strong feeling within myself that there was a strong likelihood of an underlying psychosis, and that was one of the reasons why I felt a Rorschach test was very important.

Q—What is the purpose of it? You still haven't told us what they were . . . you found in addition to the Rorschach test.

A—. . . I have given you the symptoms of schizophrenia. I have told you they occur in all degrees and severity.

Q—In other people?

A—I said they occur in all degrees of severity. Sometimes they are so out-spoken any layman would know it; other times they are so hidden, so difficult to penetrate, that a skilled psychiatrist is needed.

Q—Doctor, I am not asking what other patients may show. I am asking what Gibbs showed to you. . . .

A—And I have told you, to the best of my ability.

Coldly, Ranck said, "I have yet to hear it."

Judge Wissler broke in gently, "I understand his definition."

Dr. Strecker said, "You wouldn't want me to say he had symptoms he didn't have, or that I didn't find?"

Ranck made a gesture of impatience. "My question is directed solely to what he says he found in this defendant that fitted that definition. I have heard emotional immaturity, inadequate emotional reaction——"

"Those are the things you will hear from me," Dr. Strecker interjected.

The Judge said, "He has stated he does think this defendant knew the difference between right and wrong, but he has latent schizophrenia. Now, then, he has defined what he thinks he has along that line."

"If you mean is he a textbook case, he isn't, no, but many are not," Dr. Strecker said.

Ranck persisted, "I have heard only one statement —emotional immaturity."

The Doctor shook his head. "Personality deviation, emotional immaturity, emotional dependency, inadequacy of emotional reaction."

Ranck asked him to define each. Dr. Strecker said that "personality deviation" meant "a considerable departure in the pattern of human personality as based on average personality." He said Gibbs showed this by his emotional immaturity. Ranck asked him to repeat this, and to define "emotional immaturity." The Doctor said that it meant "that the individual has not grown up even on a minimum basis in his emotional life and stature and emotional reactions, and is not capable, and never does so sufficiently to accomplish the personal responsibilities of adult life, and falls down in them." Ranck asked how Gibbs had fallen down. The Doctor answered that Gibbs had never come, in school, anywhere near the capability of his mind. Ranck:

Q—Would you say lazy people in school are emotionally immature?

A—That may or may not be.

Q—You are basing that on the fact he didn't use that I.Q. . . . ?

A—I am basing it on him not having made a go of his life.

Q—In what way has he not?

A—He is here today in Court.

Q—Now, Doctor—

A—I am beginning at the end. His marriage, I believe, was a failure. He was unable to break away from his mother. His sex life, in my opinion, was one of inadequacy and immaturity. I think in all the relations of his life . . . except in the ordinary companionship with some college friends, he was inadequate and ineffective.

Q—I believe it was testified this defendant admitted he was a badly spoiled brat and he lost his temper?

A—. . . He said it to your psychiatrist.

*

Q—Let's suppose he is a badly spoiled brat and lacks emotional control. Would you consider he fits into the pattern of what has been previously described as immature or undeveloped by virtue of lack of discipline on the part of his parents?

A—You mean would the kind of reactions you described, and that he said he was a badly spoiled brat, the whole picture, would that help produce emotional immaturity? Very definitely it would, and it does . . .

Q—Are such people called schizophrenics?

A—No, sir. We are talking now about . . . emotionally immature people.

Q—Would you call emotionally immature people schizophrenics?

A—No, but a great many schizophrenics have been emotionally immature people.

*

Q—Does this defendant, in your opinion, have psychosis?

A—Yes, sir.

Q—Explain psychosis.

A—Psychosis is practically the equivalent of mental disease.

Q—Let's go one step farther. Is mental disease insanity?

A—That is the legal name for medical disease. I have to say that because psychiatrists don't use the word insane.

Q—It is not, however, a form of psychosis that makes one insane in the eyes of the law?

A—That is right.

Q—You could have someone with psychosis who under the Pennsylvania law would be held responsible for his acts?

A—The mere fact that a person has psychosis doesn't mean that he is legally insane. It does always bring up the degree of responsibility.

Q—What kind of psychosis?

A—You mean in this defendant, of being insane or not?

Q—Yes.

A—I think he has schizophrenia which is one of the recognized forms of mental illness. I don't believe he completely meets the conditions of legal insanity . . . nor completely meets the conditions of the McNaughton rule, completely unable to distinguish between right and wrong. I want to be sure that you understand that is my opinion. I am not saying anything else.

Ranck walked over to the Commonwealth's table, secured what appeared to be a small stick, and went back to the stand.

Q—Now, Doctor, I show you a ruler. Now let us assume that the bottom of this ruler as it touches the witness stand here has reached the level of what we call legal insanity. Let's assume the top of the ruler where you have your finger is a normal person. Where do you place Edward Gibbs?

*

A—I think that is a very interesting way of putting it. In reference to those two points, of course, this is just a guess.

Q—I understand. If I could think of some other way to ask this question, I would.

A—Meaning again, up here a great majority of people would be grouped at the top, normal, legal insanity here (*indicating*) I would say I would put him about, this is just a guess, about 6¼.

Q—He would be a little bit closer to insanity in the legal sense than your completely normal?

A—Yes.

Q—Halfway between, approximately?

A—A little more than halfway.

Q—Where did you put him?

A—I said 6¼, but I don't know. It is an interesting way of looking at it.

Brown stepped in. "You said before—Mr. Ranck stopped you—but you said you didn't think the judges were still interpreting the McNaughton rule in all its strictness——"

Dr. Strecker nodded. "I did say that."

Brown said, "What I want to ask this witness is this: it will be covered by Your Honor—ten years ago, or approximately that, prior to the recent Supreme Court decisions, a psychiatrist was not allowed to testify other than to say a man is insane or isn't insane as legally defined by the Supreme Court, which means, does he know the difference between right and wrong. Psychiatrists are now permitted to testify, and the Supreme Court has so ruled they may testify to mental disease not amounting to insanity which impairs the defendant's mental processes and which are allowed in evidence in mitigation of the punishment."

Ranck objected to this; the Judge said he would cover it in his charge. Dr. Strecker stepped down from the stand, in obvious relief.

Dr. Eleanor Ross, of Philadelphia, psychologist, diplomate of the Rorschach Institute, was called by

Brown. She testified that she had given Gibbs a Rorschach at the Lancaster County Prison on February 8. After getting these facts, Brown asked her to briefly explain the Rorschach test. She said:

The Rorschach is one of a number of . . . projective devices for evaluating personality. They are tests in active use . . . in practically all of our mental hospitals. The idea back of the test, to put it very simply, is that in most situations people are inclined to react in a learned way, in modes they have learned from other people and the ways they think are right and wrong modes of behavior. In other words, they do what they think is expected of them. Now, all our ideas of what people are like are gained from watching, from noting what they do. You can tell what a woman is like by watching her wash dishes. You can tell what sort a man is by keeping your eyes on him while he is driving a car, but in most of these situations people do things the way they learned, either directly or by copying their parents or other people around. If you can set up an unstructured situation, that is one where there is no right or wrong way of reacting, a situation in which the person whom you are working upon is entitled to do, to react, according to his own way of doing things, you get what amounts to an amassing of various personality traits and the Rorschach is the only one of these projective tests which tend to do that . . .

*

MR. BROWN: Give the results of that Rorschach test.

A—The Rorschach which Mr. Gibbs produced was a very brief one . . . very guarded and very cautious. . . . He tended to cling very much to the obvious, seeming considerably unwilling to give anything but the obviously and patently correct responses. However, even with those he tended . . . to give observations which other people do not give, while leaving out common ones which other people do give, and in spite of the extreme caution there were sufficient slips in logic which occurred even though being extremely careful to appear logical and correct in his responses—in spite of that, slips in logic occurred which are quite erratic and indicative of early disintegration of his mental processes. From the intellectual angle, the Rorschach showed that the general function was below that which would be expected of a person of his known ability. When I say his ability, I mean he does have an I.Q. of 117 . . . he is a college student. This is not a record that would be produced by a college student; it is much poorer. In addition to queer specifications, I noted the absence of the usual specifications. One card, which is practically never rejected by normal persons, he rejected completely. That is, he said he saw nothing on it. It is almost impossible for a normal person not to see anything in this instance. In another instance he gave completely bizarre, illogical, erratic responses. Finally, when shown the response which most people give, things very common, he didn't see these things. He refused to admit they were there. From the emotional angle the Rorschach revealed he is a very passive, dependent sort of person who seems very insecure as a man and seems to very much doubt, have a great many doubts, as to his own masculinity. He showed bland indifference to emotions. . . . He was very much disturbed when he ran up against strong stimulation on a card, blocked completely, was unable to give responses, said the card looked like nothing. I felt that on the basis of the Rorschach he was extremely immature and I will define what I mean by immature in addition to what Dr. Strecker has said. I feel as we grow up—a little child reacts very much in accordance with what his own desires are, he lives according to his own desires for pleasure . . . and as he grows older he learns to take into consideration far more distant goals. In order to do that he has to utilize imagination, he has to be able to visualize this distant goal, has to be able to get a certain amount of feeling from within himself as to be able to withdraw, as it were, from the rest of the world when beset by trouble to figure things out for himself, working problems through before taking action. In the Rorschach Mr. Gibbs shows no capability whatsoever to do this. I felt that he showed some anxiety, though not a great deal, and it impressed me as not being a neurotic type of anxiety. The neurotic type of defense did not appear to be present, and on the basis of that I felt this represents an early schizophrenic state. Now, I pointed out in my report here . . . that there was a great deal of façade present, front, that he was able under most circumstances and most situations to react in a normal fashion, but underlying this was the capacity for erratic, irrelevant things, and for the bland reason as described by Dr. Strecker as schizophrenia.

Q—Does that sum up your opinion?

A— . . . do you wish me to put in the material from Dr. Klopfer?

Ranck objected swiftly: "He is not competent."

Miss Ross was referring to some additional material which she and Dr. Strecker had obtained. Dr. Strecker had previously described this to Brown in a letter as follows:

"In order that the interpretation of the test should be made without bias . . . I arranged for Dr. Ross to send the test, sealed and with no identification of the subject thereof . . . to Dr. Bruno Klopfer, PhD., Director of the Rorschach Institute and Society for Projective Techniques, and Associate Professor of Clinical Psychology, University of California, Los Angeles. . . . In my opinion, Dr. Klopfer is the foremost man in this field in America. . . . Dr. Klopfer believed and reported that the test was made on an individual who was either recovering from schizophrenia or someone who was developing this form of mental disease or insanity. . . . After he had made his interpretation, Dr. Klopfer then read the history. He was then at particular pains to determine whether possibly the Rorschach responses indicate epilepsy or hysteria, or possibly organic disease of the brain. After weighing all of these considerations carefully, Dr.

Klopfer's final conclusion was, 'I feel even more sure now of an underlying psychotic condition' . . ."

Ranck had declared that Dr. Klopfer's letter not competent to be admitted as testimony since he was not present, and after some little commotion, his statements were disallowed. Miss Ross then read her summary:

> . . . It is my impression that this man is in an early schizophrenic state though with a good deal of residual reality contact which is probably adequate to conceal his erratic thinking under most circumstances. This psychosis appears in a basically immature, passive, ineffective person.
>
> Q—Did you feel . . . there was present the potentiality for psychotically motivated actions?
>
> A—I did.
>
> Q—What do you mean by that?
>
> A—I believe when I say psychotically— I said unconsciously motivated action. I feel under certain circumstances, in the first strong emotional stimulation, this man could react in response to an unconscious motive rather than a conscious motive. In other words, he could react, do something, for a reason he is completely unaware of.

As he had with Dr. Strecker, Ranck moved in on Dr. Ross immediately.

> Q—What would that emotional stimulation be, applied to this case?
>
> A—I don't know, applied to this case.

*

Q—Miss Ross, is it possible to get a violent emotional turn to color or even distort a psychological evaluation such as the Rorschach test?

A—The expert evidence in that direction is we do get variances in test results which reflect current moods to some extent, but basically the personality pattern is never altered.

Ranck asked if in Dr. Ross' opinion Gibbs had been in a state of tension and anxiety at the time she had examined him. She said that he had.

Q—Isn't the general theory of the Rorschach test, Miss Ross, that in effect it is a mirror of the human mind?

A—Yes, it is.

Q—Would that be a simple way of trying to describe it? We have black thoughts, we look at the ink blots, we will reveal what we think. In fact, we give away what we have up here (*indicating head*), through the interpretation of the ink blots?

A—Yes, that is correct.

Miss Ross, at Ranck's request, produced a set of the Rorschach ink blots. He held them up for the Jury to see, explaining that each was numbered on the back.

Q—Now, will you explain to the Jury how that ink blot was made, if you know?

A—Surely. These are photographs representing the original ink blots which were devised by Dr. Rorschach in Switzerland in 1910, or thereafter. They were made by splashing ink on paper, in the center, folding the

220

paper together so that it would smear, opening it up so that you would get a design more or less symmetrical on each side. These blots were selected from many thousands which had been made to start off with because these particular blots seemed to stimulate people more than others that had been made.

Q—You mean stimulate the imagination so that somebody may see something in here other persons wouldn't see?

A—That is right.

As though administering the test himself, Ranck now began holding up the ink blot cards. He came finally to No. 8. Miss Ross said that was the one Gibbs had rejected. Ranck:

Q—State to the jury what, in your opinion, would be the normal diagnosis of the horror picture. This is in three different shades of pink, different colors?

A—Sort of a grey blue, pink, sort of an orchid color.

Q—What would you consider a normal reaction?

A—The most common reaction is to see animals on the side here, animals walking or crawling on something. That is possibly the most common response to all cards. Mr. Gibbs didn't see it.

*

Q—Was your diagnosis of this defendant gathered exclusively from his responses on being shown these various cards?

A—Yes. May I explain a little bit about how an analysis is made? In addition to the content of the response, that is, the thing which is seen, which is of some importance, major emphasis is placed on the interpretation, on the way in which the individual is able to project movement into the cards, that is, to see people or animals in action, the way in which he uses the color, either in a violent, imaginative way, seeing floods, fires, things of that type, or more spontaneously, plants, sea life, something a little bit gentler than blood and fire, and the various ways they mention the shaded nuances, and use . . . them to give the effect of surface appearance or texture or whether they appear small differences, as smoke, mist, fog or something of that type. Analysis of all is done in a very methodical sort of way. Every single response is scored according to what area of the card is used, in what way these various determinates, movement, color, shading and form are introduced, as well as to what the actual content of the responses is, and we have any number of expert data verifying the validity of independent items in the Rorschach. . . .

*

Q—Well, it has been testified that this defendant took psychology in college and was failing. . . . Would the Rorschach test be something that would be taken up in an ordinary psychology course?

A—Ordinarily it is not taken up until graduate level. However, it is done usually in post-graduate study.

Q—In your opinion, this man as a college student, would he be likely to have heard of the Rorschach test?

A—He may or may not have. I asked him.

Q—Was there any indication made as to the purpose of this? Did he say it was a personality evaluation test?

A—No.

Q—What did you say to him?

A—He had been informed of the examination by Dr. Strecker and Mr. Brown, and it had been completely introduced when I came into the room. I asked him when he came in if he had read anything about the Rorschach in the newspapers, knowing there had been some articles in conjunction with the publicity about the crime. He said, "No," and at that point went on to discuss his interest in reading, complained he had not been allowed to have novels, went on to discuss various novels he had read. I felt this was rather inappropriate to that sort of thing.

Q—Then you showed him the cards, one, two, three?

A—Yes, I started out. I told him—as a matter of fact it is a little difficult to remember what I did tell him—I said, "You know about this test?" He said, "Yes, I do." Then I explained how the ink blots were made, we started off, he gave responses, and I recorded it.

223

Court was adjourned until nine thirty A.M. the next day. By now Brown was beginning to worry, but he still felt that Gibbs had made an excellent appearance and that both Dr. Strecker and Dr. Ross had established evidence of his abnormality. Ranck, on the other hand, was certain he had created some doubts as to the reliability of both. He and William Storb had a long conference that evening. Each felt that there must be some device by means of which they could nail down their case. Neither could think of anything. They were hoping that Dr. Baldwin L. Keyes, their rebuttal psychiatrist, would aid materially, but they were not certain of the effect he would have upon the jury. At four the next morning, Storb awakened suddenly from a sound sleep. There, in his mind, was what he and Ranck had been seeking. He could not restrain himself from calling Ranck and announcing it. They used it in Court almost immediately the next day. Brown first called Dr. French J. Friedlin, who testified as to the dinner party at the Gibbs home during which Gibbs had lost his temper so violently. Ranck cross-examined Dr. Friedlin briefly, almost carelessly. Then, without warning, he recalled Dr. Strecker to the stand for further cross-examination. Dr. Strecker seemed puzzled. Brown, at counsel table, was going through his papers, preparing for the next witness.

Ranck, in a voice that rang through the room, said, "Doctor, I have just one question. Do you feel that this defendant, Edward Gibbs, might kill again?"

Dr. Strecker hesitated only for a moment. Then he said, "I think it is possible that he might. You couldn't be sure."

The effect upon the Jury and the audience was plainly visible. There are many who believe that this question decided the case. Ranck, in recalling it, said, "It was one

224

of those perfect questions—either way it was answered, it didn't matter. It was the kind of perfect question they tell you about in law school." The affirmative answer was damaging, but a negative answer would have been equally so; Ranck then would have submitted Dr. Strecker to another session such as he had the day before. Brown, recalling the incident, says he was totally unprepared for the question. It caught him so by surprise he did not object, as he perhaps should have done.

When the excitement had died down, Brown called George Dolan, of Salem, New Jersey, explaining that he hoped to prove with Dolan's testimony that Gibbs had been "terribly upset and affected, and mentally disturbed" at the time he washed out of pilot training. Ranck offered no objection. Dolan first testified as to his service with Gibbs, and then Brown led him to Gibbs' failure. Brown:

> Q—What was his reaction?
> A—Well, Ed's reaction, when he didn't make the grade, he was terribly crushed and upset, he wept, in fact he was just completely, well, I don't just know how to phrase it, he was sunk. He had his heart and mind set on making the grade on this thing, and Ed didn't pass. There were several others that didn't, also, but Ed had put his best foot on this thing and it had fallen through, and he was crushed.

Ranck's cross-examination was very brief. He asked if there were several others who failed at the same time Gibbs had, and Dolan said there were. Ranck then offered the Ink Blots to be admitted as evidence.

Brown said, "The defendant rests."

As rebuttal witness, Ranck now called Dr. Baldwin Longstreth Keyes, of Philadelphia, a psychiatrist, Professor of Psychiatry at Jefferson Medical College, and consultant to several other institutions, among them the Veterans Bureau and Philadelphia General Hospital. Dr. Keyes, a man of medium height with tightly brushed white hair and sharp blue eyes, said that he had been practicing in psychiatry since 1919, that he had been a colleague of Dr. Strecker, and a Colonel in the Medical Department during World War II. Dr. Keyes stated that he had examined Gibbs on March 10, 1950, for two hours, making a physical examination, and a neurological examination, and a psychiatric evaluation. Ranck asked Dr. Keyes first if Gibbs had outlined anything to him that had not been covered in Dr. Strecker's testimony, or if anything had been outlined in a different way. It was Ranck's design to have Dr. Keyes show that while Gibbs was unquestionably emotionally immature, and perhaps even a disturbed person, he was nevertheless sane in the strictest interpretation of the law. This Dr. Keyes proceeded to do calmly and scientifically. He first read a long statement, the gist of which was that Gibbs was not at all an unusual fellow; that he had been spoiled by his family, and that was the root of his difficulty in adjusting to the world. He said he thought Gibbs' sexual experiences were not unusual; he said that Gibbs' Army career had been shaped in part by the fact that he suffered a comedown from his superior stature around Pitman. He said that Gibbs broke down while describing the events of January 10, but that otherwise he was very co-operative and friendly. At the close of the statement, Ranck began questioning his witness.

Q—Dr. Keyes, you heard Dr. Strecker on the stand yesterday?
A—Yes, sir.

*

Q—Do you agree with that diagnosis of latent schizophrenia?

A—I don't feel that was the picture, clinically, that I saw, no, sir.

*

Q—Now, why do you disagree . . . ?

A—Well, I felt the diagnosis of schizophrenia as Dr. Strecker described it, rests on certain definite symptoms such as no emotional tone. . . . It depends certainly on personality forces such as seclusion, perhaps suspicion, perhaps wishing to withdraw from people a little bit, staying away from friends rather than going to friends, leading an isolated existence, following the usual personality traits of a schizophrenic who is withdrawing from reality, gravitating into a far world of his own where he begins to get delusions, fantasies, and lives in a fanciful little world he created, but I didn't feel this gentleman shows any of these symptoms. He did show emotional immaturity, I think there is no question about that. . . . It is a very common finding in a family where one child gets too much attention. . . .

Q—Did you get that from seeing how he acted, or what?

A—I thought from the way he behaved while talking to him, the nature of his discussion, and from what he disclosed to me of himself, I thought his reactions on an emotional plane were perfectly normal to the circumstances in which he found himself, and to the subject under discussion at the time. He was crying when we talked about his mother, etc., and upset, properly and appropriately, it seemed to me, when we were discussing this tragedy.

Q—Now, Doctor, would you give us in as simple language as you can your diagnosis of this defendant from what you saw in the Lancaster County Prison and from what you know of his case history?

A—Well, he seemed to me like so many other boys who have had the experience of emotional immaturity, showed a great deal of frustration in trying to do something he didn't want to do. Therefore, he showed what we refer to as personality deviation in the direction of emotional immaturity, but that was as far as I felt I could go on the basis of calling him a sick person. I think he was a disturbed person.

＊

Q—You are familiar with the Pennsylvania rule on legal insanity?

A—Yes, sir.

Q—In your opinion, Doctor, is this defendant legally sane?

A—Yes, he is legally sane.

Q—Is there any question in your mind about that?

A—No doubt about it.

Q—Now, Doctor Keyes, I show you this ruler which we used in the course of the examination of Dr. Strecker yesterday. Now, assuming the top of the witness stand, the 12 inch mark, to represent legal insanity, and where I have my finger at the top of the ruler to be the normal person, where would you place this defendant, Edward Gibbs?

A—From a legal standpoint he is up at the top of the level of your ruler in the sense he is not legally insane.

MR. BROWN: I didn't get that.

THE WITNESS: As far as legally insane, he is not legally insane.

Q—That is not quite my question. This is a normal person at the top, this is a person here who is legally insane. Between legal insanity and absolute normalcy, where would we place this defendant?

A—From the standpoint of responsibility he is the same as anyone else, in knowing right from wrong. From the standpoint of having personality deviations, which we call emotional immaturity, he would be somewhat below normal.

Q—About how far?

A—I would guess about two inches, not on a sick level.

Brown began to cross-examine the witness.

Q—I want to get that a little better. You heard Dr. Strecker say yesterday that he placed the defendant . . . a little over six inches below normal?

A—Yes, sir.

Q—You place it about 2 inches; is that it?

A—Roughly. It is a hard thing to measure by because you are talking about two things. Which one——

Q—Dr. Strecker said it was a guess. You say the same thing?

A—Right.

Q—You admit he is below the normal level?

A—That is right.

*

Q—Doctor, I understood you to say you studied under Dr. Strecker?

A—At the Pennsylvania Hospital for 4 years, the first 4 years. We worked there together ever since.

Q—Doctor, the extent of your examination consisted of what took place in the . . . Prison on March 10th; is that right?

A—I spent approximately a little over 2 hours with Mr. Gibbs on Friday, March 10th. I didn't see him before and not again until Court here, every day here.

*

Q—You didn't cause any examinations to be made?

A—No, sir, I had access to the examinations you had done.

Under Brown's searching cross-examination, Dr. Keyes admitted his high regard for the competence of Drs. Strecker and Ross. He said that he, too, had made a report in writing to the District Attorney after his examination of Gibbs. Brown produced this report and turned to Page 7:

Q—Now, Doctor . . . you say there is no indication of any form of a psychosis, and the only clinical evidence of an abnormal personality is that of his immature dependency on his family, and his inability to maintain disciplinary control over himself as regards frustrations and emotional controls. You said that?

A—Yes, sir.

Q—You said in the paragraph before he was normal, hadn't you?

A—Yes, I think he is normal except for being an emotionally immature person.

Q—Isn't one of the chief signs of mental disturbance inability to control yourself?

A—Well, of course . . . it depends on the type of sickness you have.

*

Q—There are some, aren't there, some in which the inability to control oneself is a serious mental weakness?

A—I wouldn't call it a serious mental weakness. I would call that a sign of weakness in any of us.

Q—What kind?

A—Emotional control, weakness, if you will.

Q—And then you say his inability to maintain disciplinary control over himself is evident in his personality as regards frustrations and emotional controls?

A—Yes. I think what he shows is the evidence of never having had to discipline himself, of having everything handed to him, accepting it freely, and being very much upset, such as having temper tantrums when he didn't get what he wanted. He still has times of being upset, where he loses his temper when he doesn't get what he wants.

Q—How do you reconcile that? You stated that he is completely—showed normal emotional responses to the subjects you discussed and behaved normally in every way?

A—That is right.

Q—That isn't consistent with your second finding?

A—Yes, quite consistent, because during the time he talked to me he was not facing any undue frustration . . . He was perfectly free and in entire contact with reality, mentally entirely clear, knew exactly what was going on, told his story well in sequence. If he digressed, he would come back to the subject matter without any trouble, certainly nothing wrong with his intellectual processes.

*

Q—Now, you say he does have emotional immaturity? What was that?

A—Personality deviations, showing immaturity.

Q—Will you explain that?

A—As I said just a minute ago, that is a term used to describe persons, who when they fail to develop complete independence of his, away from his family, independence from mother control, the cutting of the apron strings sort of thing, he fails to develop complete discipline at all times, control of himself from the standpoint of his emotions. I said there are times—

Q—When he can't hold control?

A—He could, but hasn't learned to accept it as a normal person, for himself.

Q—Now, Doctor . . . you say, "It might be well to consider the possibility that Miss Baker's conversation about graduation stirred up Mr. Gibbs in an unadmitted hostility toward his mother"—I guess you mean unconscious?

A—Yes.

Q— . . . That was your finding?

A—That wasn't a finding. I raised that as a question for argument.

*

Brown now brought up the Harnish cottage. He referred again to Dr. Keyes' statement.

Q—Then you said you didn't think he would go to such a remote place?

A—I didn't quite say that.

Q—If this was so?

A—If this was so, it would have been an unconscious motive and he would not have taken the pains to go to such a distance and such a secluded spot, nor would he have waited until she started to talk about the beautiful scenery. I thought he would do it at the time when she was talking about the things that upset him, if it upset him, such as graduation, but he told me her conversation didn't upset him.

Q—But . . . you say that talk about graduation which was conducted could have been causing frustration and emotional disturbance?

A—Yes, I raised the question . . . that is one of the possibilities to consider, but I felt it was not valid here because the conversation, he said, did not upset him in any way, and at the final moment the conversation was about the scenery and nothing about graduation.

*

Q—You are basing it on what he said, aren't you?

A—And how he behaved while he told me about it.

Q—And if he told you that did cause him to get very much disturbed and upset, you would have thought that conversation had a great deal——

A—No, not in the way this occurred. Those things are done quickly, and are an unconscious reaction, but this was a long continuing chain of circumstances, from the way he met her, the time to drive out there, coming around the circle, looking at the scenery. If there was any surging of that sort, it would have happened a long time before.

Q—But, Doctor, it could have been welling up in his mind and heart while driving along?

A—I don't think so, when they stopped and looked over the scenery.

Q—Is it possible?

A—I don't think it is possible.

Q—Aren't you saying there, in effect . . .

that Gibbs had no conscious motive for his criminal act, it could have come on him anywhere?

A—No . . . I am not sure he didn't have a conscious motive for his criminal act.

Q—Might it have been he had no concious motive?

A—I don't know that, from his story.

*

Q—In other words, he didn't know why he killed Miss Baker?

A—No, he didn't say. I said *I* don't know why he killed Miss Baker.

Q—You don't know whether he had any conscious motive?

A—I didn't find out what that was.

Brown began to attack Dr. Keyes' diagnosis of Gibbs' condition as one of "personality disorders, with exaggerated personality reactions." He asked the psychiatrist how he reconciled that with his previously stated opinion that Gibbs was about two inches below normal on the ruler. Dr. Keyes said again that they were talking about two different things; that Gibbs had normal intelligence, which would have placed him at the top, but that since he had a personality defect, he was "a little off." But, said Dr. Keyes, he would be "normal" in everything except his "emotional tone." Brown:

Q—What do you mean, he was normal?

A—I mean he has normal maturity, normal control of himself under average circumstances, mingles well with people, led his life at college like anybody else, apparently nobody noticed anything wrong with him except he has a more or less an explosive temper, you might call it.

Q—So he might look all right to everybody, but he isn't 100%?

A—I think we all have some defect, if studied in detail.

Q—You mean to say everybody in this Court Room has some defect?

A—I think we all fall into certain personality classifications.

Q—You wouldn't think everybody falls into the personality classification of Gibbs?

A—I think the circumstances are a little bit different. I don't think he would have been examined had this not happened.

Brown read Dr. Keyes' report that dealt with Gibbs' Army experiences. He asked if it were not true that Gibbs had had a difficult time; the Doctor said that in his opinion it was not too difficult. Then Brown went on to the part of the report that discussed Gibbs' and his wife's habit of practicing interruptus.

Q—Isn't it true psychiatrists agree this is emotionally disturbing?

A—I talked to him a little bit about that. It didn't seem to disturb him.

Q—Isn't it true psychiatrists generally agree that it is a great emotional experience, practicing withdrawal?

A—I think it depends entirely on the individual, on the amount of release he gains. You can't pin it down to one.

Q—What is the feeling of the average man?

A—Well, I think we all investigate it in our histories and then talk to the patient to determine how much it has affected him.

Q—What is the normal effect?

A—In many instances it doesn't make too much difference in some people. Others get a bit tense, anxious, depressed, perhaps irritable toward each other, etc. In some instances there is just lessening of interest in the act.

Q—It causes irritability toward each other in many instances?

A—In this instance he told me it didn't seem to have any effect on either except to lessen interest in the sex act, and holding off, waiting to have a child, which was part of his wanting to have a job.

Brown now directed his attention to the part of the report which dealt with Gibbs' anxiety and depression during the holidays and just prior to his crime. Dr. Keyes testified that Gibbs had told him of these feelings specifically. Brown went on:

Q—The paragraph . . . where he said he was frustrated—"This frustration was inside of me and had to come out. I asked if this had anything to do with the Baker episode, and he said, 'No, nothing at all.'" Why did you ask that?

A—I was trying to find out whether there was some significance to it.

Q—He said there wasn't?

A— . . . he didn't think it made too much difference.

Q—But . . . in your mind it probably

had something to do with the crime? That is the reason you asked that?

A—Yes, I thought it might be possible.

*

Q—Could anybody tell, Doctor, in psychosis, when an unconscious motive will react or take place?

A—I don't think you can unless you know the patient pretty well and know what kind of things stir him.

*

Brown turned to Gibbs' family background, with particular reference to the mental illness of the maternal great-grandmother and the alcoholic uncle. Dr. Keyes said he did not believe that either relative's condition had much bearing on Gibbs' present situation. Brown asked him to define psychosis; he said, "Mental illness, in which a person is unable to handle reality." He then continued, under questioning, to explain that he did not believe Gibbs to be psychotic at all, or to even "approach psychosis." He said that Gibbs had "pent-up emotions." He continued to insist that he found "a normal emotional tone" in Gibbs reaction to his interview. Then he agreed that both he and Dr. Strecker had found Gibbs "emotionally immature." Finally, he said that the fundamental difference between himself and Dr. Strecker was on the subject of Gibbs' schizophrenia. Ranck arose to ask several additional questions.

Q—Doctor, you and Dr. Strecker both found immaturity?

A—That is right.

238

Q—In your opinion is that sufficient on which to base a diagnosis of schizophrenia?

A—Certainly not.

Q—What else?

A—I think you have to have other clinical evidence of schizophrenia.

Q—How much?

A—You have some traits of personality, withdrawal from reality, incoherent thinking, bizarre behavior, delusions, many times.

Brown came back to the stand.

Q—You heard Miss Ross say he had bizarre behavior?

A—I thought she understood his behavior was out of proportion to the situation in which he found himself, which . . . I explained was a defense mechanism used in times of stress.

Q— . . . You agree he was able to distinguish between right and wrong?

A—That is right.

*

Everyone agreed that Brown's cross-examination had been no less searching than Ranck's previous tilt with Dr. Strecker. But it was also felt that Dr. Keyes had been a more direct, and therefore more impressive, witness.

The District Attorney had one final question for Dr. Keyes. "Do I understand you to say that legally this man is fully responsible for his actions?"

"That is right," said Dr. Keyes, and stepped down from the stand.

Ranck offered a number of witnesses in rebuttal who would testify that they had known Gibbs over a period of time and had never heard nor seen him say or do anything which led them to believe he was of unsound mind. Brown objected, and the offer was disallowed.

The evidence was closed.

Brown's closing speech came next. Friends said he did very well; today he claims he did not do as well as he might have. If there was a second victim in the Gibbs case, it was this attorney; even today he sometimes relives the entire affair in his mind, questioning his own conduct, wishing he had it to do over. Yet it is difficult to believe that, in the face of Gibbs' stubborn, sick silence, he could have done more with the task he set himself. One of the things he most reproaches himself for is the closing speech. He used his voice to the fullest extent of its powers . . . and in the middle, it failed him. He had to speak nearly forty minutes. Water did not help. By law, neither the defense counsel's summary nor that of the District Attorney are contained in the court record; there is, therefore, no exact transcript of what he said. He began by saying that the defendant admitted the seriousness of the crime. "I would be derelict in my duty if I didn't say that Gibbs committed a serious offense. But he was the victim of many things welling up in his heart." Reviewing the evidence that had been presented, he said there was no proof that Gibbs had ever said, as the police had testified, that Marian Baker was hard to kill and that she didn't want to die.

"That is the only testimony," said Brown, "which would indicate coldness and callousness. That was not in his statement." His voice rose. "How in the world would such a damaging statement be missed? In fairness to the defendant I believe you must expung this from your mind." He became angry. "The Commonwealth attempted to bring sex into this case. There is no scintilla of evidence

240

of a sex attack on the case. Eliminate this, too, from your mind."

Brown went on to review the emotional strain Gibbs had been under. He once more went over the medical testimony. He said, "If Gibbs was mentally upset it requires careful consideration in your deliberations. It is indisputable evidence . . . You, the jury, have the power to mitigate the punishment. You must find the elements of wilfulness, deliberation and premeditation to return a first degree murder verdict." At the close, his voice dropped. "I ask for you Divine guidance in reaching a verdict," he said. He wiped his head and sat down.

Ranck's speech shocked some of the spectators in its extreme bitterness. He spoke for fifty minutes, never once relenting in intensity. Facing Gibbs for an instant, he said, "In our opinion, as was stated at the opening of the case, this is one of first degree murder. It is the only degree of felonious homicide we intend to discuss with you. . . . A human life has been forfeited. . . . This is a deadly serious case. The facts show that it was a wilful, deliberate, and premeditated killing. This case is the People vs. Edward L. Gibbs, including Marian Baker, her family, her friends." His voice became contemptuous. "Gibbs was not insane," he stated, flatly, "he was devilishly clever. It is frightening to think how close this fellow came to getting away with this crime."

After a pause, Ranck went on, "Marian Baker's lips are sealed, and other than some exhibits, all we have is Eddie's story. According to that, she said, 'Isn't that a beautiful view?' and then he killed her. I don't go for that kind of a story. . . . The State need not prove intent in such a case as this . . . but we think he went there and made a sexual advance to Miss Baker. He was married. She was an engaged girl. She indicated she would tell the college authorities or his wife. Then he tries to quiet her. He kills her. I believe that afternoon, seated in the car, he placed his arm around her shoulder, grabbed her panties and garter belt and that she yelled and attempted to flee . . ." Ranck held up the garter belt. He next tried to make it seem that Gibbs had been lying when he stated that he had dragged Marian Baker by the arms, legs, and head. "When the body was found, Miss Baker's coat was pulled off one shoulder," Ranck stated. "If he had dragged her by the arms, the coat would have been pulled back on her shoulder." He pulled his own coat down, and pulled it back. This was the first in a series of physical gestures which must have had a powerful effect upon the jury. When he launched into his closing sentences, he showed the jury the pictures that had been admitted as evidence. He waved the lug wrench in the air. When he picked up Marian Baker's underwear, he wiped off his hands afterward, "as if," as the *New Era* reporter wrote, "to eradicate the suggestions which they implied." He declared, in speaking of the psychiatric testimony in Gibbs' behalf, that it was more than possible that Gibbs had faked his reactions in the tests and examinations.

"If a crime of this nature does not warrant the supreme penalty under Pennsylvania law, I can't conjure up one which would," Ranck said in conclusion. His final sentence was "God give you wisdom."

At three five P.M., Judge Wissler began his charge to the jury. In part, it read as follows:

The case requires of the court, and of you, members of the jury, the discharge of a solemn and responsible duty cast upon the court and the jury. The fate of the defendant on the one hand, and on the other, the maintenance of the law

242

made and ordained to shield and protect life, are committed to us; and the discharge of our respective duties to the one and to the other, is required of us alike, according to our best judgment, under the solemn sanction of an oath. It is the court's duty to state to you the law and to indicate to you the questions for your decision which arise in its application. It is your duty to apply the law, as you receive it from the court, to the facts as you have received them from witnesses, and heard them discussed by counsel, and so make up your verdict.

It is the court's earnest desire that you may be guided to conclusions which will discharge the solemn obligations of the oath taken by you all . . . and that your deliberations may result in "a true deliverance between the Commonwealth and the prisoner."

At the common law murder is described to be, when a person of sound memory and discretion unlawfully kills any reasonable creature in being and under the peace of the Commonwealth, with malice aforethought, express or implied. The distinguishing criterion of murder is malice aforethought. But it is not malice in its ordinary understanding alone, a particular ill-will, a spite or a grudge. Malice is a legal term, implying much more. It comprehends not only a particular ill-will, but every case where there is wickedness of disposition, hardness of heart, cruelty, recklessness of consequences, and a mind regardless of social duty, although a particular person may not be intended to be injured. Murder, therefore, at common law embraces cases where no intent to kill existed, but where the state or frame of mind termed malice, in its legal sense, prevailed.

In Pennsylvania, the Legislature, considering that there is a manifest difference in the degree of guilt, where a deliberate intention to kill exists, and where none appears, distinguished murder into two grades, murder of the first and murder of the second degree; and provided that the jury before whom any person indicted for murder shall be tried, shall, if they find him guilty thereof, ascertain in their verdict whether it be murder of the first or murder of the second degree. Of possible kinds of murder the Act of Assembly of Pennsylvania provides . . . "All murder which shall be perpetrated by means of poison, or by lying in wait, or by any other kind of willful, deliberate, and premeditated killing, or which shall be committed in the perpetration of, or attempting to perpetrate, any arson, rape, robbery, burglary, or kidnapping, shall be murder in the first degree. All other kinds of murder shall be murder in the second degree."

You will note that under this Act murder in the first degree may be poison or lying in wait. There is no evidence of such means in this case. Or, it may be any willful, deliberate and premeditated killing.

The Judge went on to explain that in this case the murder was "willful, deliberate, and premeditated." He said that the law fixed no length of time as necessary to form the intention to kill; that the intent must be a fact determined by the jury from the evidence. Although no

244

time to decide to kill is too short a time, by law, he said, suddenness is opposed to premeditation, and the jury had to be convinced that Gibbs had had time to premeditate. He explained, too, that a person who uses a deadly weapon upon the body of another must be presumed to know that his blow is likely to kill. His charge continued:

> All murder not of the first degree is necessarily of the second degree, and includes all unlawful killing under circumstances of depravity of heart, and a disposition of mind regardless of social duty; but where no intention to kill exists or can be reasonably and fully inferred. Therefore, in all cases of murder, if no intention to kill can be inferred or collected from the circumstances, the verdict must be murder in the second degree . . .

When the Commonwealth asks for a conviction of first degree murder, the Judge continued, the burden of raising the crime from second to first is on the Commonwealth. He said that the Jury would have to decide for itself if malice did in fact exist. He then said he would relate the evidence "but briefly." He was not brief at all. The summary of the evidence ran to twenty-two pages of court record, for the Judge ran through the testimony as meticulously as a Lancaster County farmer might cull a barrel of apples. During this summary, Gibbs' head dropped on his chest. He slept soundly for about ten minutes. He had spent a sleepless night at the jail, and the courtroom was by then fairly stuffy.

After covering the testimony, the Judge cautioned the Jury again to base their findings upon their own recollection of it; to pass upon the credibility of witnesses, to take into consideration any bias, and to examine all facts and determine how far each witness was corroborated or contradicted. He reminded them that the photographs should not be allowed to inflame their minds. Then he went into the question of insanity and the law. He reminded the Jury that no formal plea of insanity had been made, and therefore the defendant's sanity was presumed. He said that evidence which creates only a "mere doubt or a reasonable doubt" was insufficient for acquittal; that the test for insanity was the ability to distinguish between right and wrong. Insanity, he said, had to be a complete defense or none at all. He went on:

> The burden of proof rests upon the Commonwealth to establish the guilt of the accused beyond a reasonable doubt. This, however, should be an honest doubt, such a reasonable doubt as fairly arises in the minds of the jury out of all or any part of the evidence; such a doubt as would cause a reasonable person or persons of ordinary prudence to hesitate to act in a manner of highest importance to himself or herself. The doubt must be substantial, not fanciful or imaginary; it must not be conjured up to avoid the performance of a disagreeable duty.
>
> If there is such doubt in your mind, the defendant is entitled to that benefit, and an acquittal. However, if the jury is satisfied beyond a reasonable doubt under all the evidence that the defendant is guilty as charged, it is your duty to convict the defendant.

The Judge next defined "reasonable doubt." He quoted The Act of Assembly which holds that a convicted murderer shall suffer death or life imprisonment. He went on:

> . . . the fixing of either the death penalty or life imprisonment is, under this Act, to be an exercise of discretion on your part . . .

He next explained that even though the law defines insanity as he had quoted it previously, the law also states that where there is evidence of mental irresponsibility or weakness, it may be offered and is admissable in possible mitigation of the penalty. This, he said, is left to the discretion of the jury. He went on:

> Therefore, . . . you are permitted to consider, if you believe the evidence . . . of mental irresponsibility or weakness . . . such as has been testified to by Dr. Strecker . . . and Miss Eleanor Ross . . . and called latent schizophrenia, which is also known as a form of deterioration or loss of intellectual faculties. You, however, will recall their testimony as to its nature.
>
> You may take this testimony into consideration . . . in fixing the degree of punishment, if you find the defendant guilty of murder in the first degree.
>
> Of course, likewise, you will take into consideration the evidence of Dr. Keyes. . . .
>
> If you are convinced beyond a reasonable doubt as to the defendant's guilt, then it is your duty to convict him and to fix the degree you are convinced beyond a reasonable doubt of which he is guilty. You may bring in one of three possible verdicts: guilty of murder in the first degree with a penalty of death; guilty of

murder in the first degree with a penalty of life imprisonment. On the other hand, if the Commonwealth has failed to convince you . . . of the guilt of the defendant on any of the charges which I have enumerated to you, then it is just as much your duty to acquit him and bring in a verdict of not guilty.

The Judge peered through his glasses first at Brown and then at Ranck. "Is there anything further, gentlemen?"

Brown rose, went forward, and handed up a paper. The Judge took it, studied it for a moment, and said to the Jury:

"In addition to the testimony regarding the mental condition of the defendant, it is the duty of the court to charge you that it is the Jury's duty to know and ascertain what kind of man this is, there being no evidence of any bad character." He paused, then began reading the points that Brown had asked to have included in his charge. He refused to read the first, which Brown had put in as a mere formality, and which said that under the law and the evidence the verdict should be "not guilty." The other points reminded the Jury that there had been no evidence of robbery, rape, or attempted rape; that a competent psychiatrist had testified that the defendant was suffering from latent psychosis, and that if the Jury believed this it would tend to prove diminished responsibility, thereby justifying a reduction of the punishment; that mental weakness should be considered in fixing the punishment; that the defendant had no prior criminal record or bad reputation should be used in mitigating the punishment; and that if the Jury felt that the killing was not willful, deliberate and premeditated, their verdict should be murder in the second degree.

Both Ranck and Storb were indignant over the in-
clusion of these points. They felt that the charge, and the
points for charge, were heavily weighted in Gibbs' favor.
The Judge ended his charge to the jury as follows:

> Now, members of the jury, you may take
> this case and give it your very careful considera-
> tion, which I know you will, all the considera-
> tion that the gravity of the crime merits, all the
> consideration that the length of the testimony
> requires. You will render your verdict un-
> affected by any bias or prejudice, or hatred
> or sympathy. Such feelings have no place in the
> deliberations and conclusions of a jury.

The District Attorney arose. "If the court please, I
ask permission to send the exhibits out with the Jury."
The Judge looked toward Brown.
"No objection, your honor."
The Judge discharged the alternate jurors, and the
twelve who were to deliberate upon the fate of Edward
Gibbs left the courtroom. They went up to the third floor
and were locked into the jury room. The clock showed
four twenty-eight, and everyone settled down, as though
sensing that the verdict would not come out for a long
time. Gibbs was removed to prison again. Reporters and
photographers took up a vigil in the downstairs corridor.
At six thirty, when two boxes of sandwiches and coffee
were taken upstairs to the jury room, the older newsmen
looked at each other in weariness. Pennsylvania state law
provides that a jury must remain locked up until a
decision has been reached. "We're in for a long one," one
man said. He was a Philadelphian. None of the Lancaster reporters said anything in response.
Judge Wissler came back from his dinner around

seven forty-five and went upstairs to his Chambers, remarking in passing that he had heard nothing. Brown and Ranck returned with their assistants. They had heard nothing.

At eight-fifty Sheriff Abe Lane answered the telephone in his office on the first floor of the courthouse. He and Deputy Elmer Zerphey immediately left for the prison to fetch Gibbs.

The ever-present crowd had gathered again. It poured into the courtroom in company with the eager newspapermen. It was not as large as it had been before. Reports later estimated it at close to one hundred people. J. Lester Gibbs and the faithful Reverend Marvin Guice were in the crowd. They took seats near the front, almost directly behind the defense attorney's table. At nine-two, the Jury came back: "Some of them had to be assisted," the *New Era* report said. "[they were] grim-faced . . . That was the first inkling of their verdict." At nine-ten, the Commonwealth and defense attorneys took their places, and a moment later Gibbs was brought in. Elmer Zerphey helped him off with his topcoat. Several of the jurors stole quick glances at him, and looked away. Judge Wissler entered, and everyone rose automatically. When they all resumed their seats, Court Clerk William Wagner stood up. He said, "Members of the Jury, have you agreed upon a verdict?"

In a chorus, they said, "We have."

Wagner went forward and took the folded paper from Charles L. Lee. He handed it to Judge Wissler, who opened it slowly. The Judge gave no sign of emotion as he read it, but there were those who thought they saw his lips press together tightly. The Judge handed the paper back to Wagner.

Now even the reporters were still. Someone coughed

nervously, and someone else echoed him. Then there was total stillness.

It seemed to take Wagner a long time to get the paper fixed in his hands for reading. When he did, he said solemnly:

"Members of the Jury, hearken unto your verdict as the Court hath recorded it. In the issue joined between the Commonwealth of Pennsylvania and Edward Lester Gibbs, you say you find the defendant, Edward Lester Gibbs, 'Guilty of Murder in the first degree, with Death Penalty,' and so say you all?"

Some of them gazed straight at the Clerk, some stared at the floor. Together they said, "We do."

Edward Gibbs' hand went to his mouth, as though to keep himself from joining in the sudden reaction, the quick gasp of amazement, that burst in the room. He could not, however, control his body; he half rose from his chair, then sank back.

Brown was asking for the Judge's attention. "If the Court please, I ask that the Jury be polled."

Judge Wissler said, "The Clerk will poll the Jury."

The newspapers stated that most of the people in the courtroom were white-faced. Tears had begun to run down Gibbs' cheeks.

The Clerk polled each juror in turn, asking, "In the issue joined between the Commonwealth of Pennsylvania and Edward Lester Gibbs, how say you?" Each answered, "Guilty of murder in the first degree, with the death penalty," or simply "Guilty, death penalty."

Once or twice, Gibbs turned to his father, his face twisted beseechingly. The father made feeble gestures of encouragement.

When the jurors had been polled, Brown and Ranck rushed to the bench. Each began speaking at the same time. The Judge, according to several reporters, looked confused; one later said, "It was obvious that he had not been expecting the jury to bring out a 'guilty with the death penalty' verdict. The thing caught him flat-footed. He didn't know what to do, and he was upset."

After a moment, the attorneys, their assistants, and Judge Wissler retired to the Judge's Chambers. They were gone at least a half hour. During this time Gibbs continued to weep and to turn to look at his pale, trembling parent. Elmer Zerphey attempted to comfort him; at one point Mrs. Helen Hair, the Court nurse, asked him if he wanted her to do anything for him. He shook his head. His expression seemed to say, "Nobody can do anything for me."

When Judge Wissler resumed his seat on the bench, he spoke like a man performing a hard task. He stated that he and the attorneys had been consulting the law as to sentencing a convicted murderer and that dealing with the mechanics of appeal. Brown had made a verbal motion for a new trial, and was to submit a written motion within a few days. The Judge dismissed the Jury without thanks and without a comment on the way they had discharged their duty. He simply told them they could go and get their pay. The jurors did not move. The Judge repeated his order, and they left.

Gibbs stumbled every few steps as he was taken handcuffed from the courtroom. At the foot of the first floor steps, the tears still flowing down his cheeks, he swung angrily at a photographer. Elmer Zerphey restrained him, murmuring words designed to calm him. A few minutes after he was taken from the courtroom, his father collapsed from the strain. A cot was brought out, and he was placed on it; it was some time before he was able to leave the courthouse.

7

The Aftermath

The trial is still a lively issue in Lancaster. The name Edward Gibbs can always be depended upon to set off a prolonged discussion, more often than not one composed of half-truths, rumors and speculation. It has become the custom of certain barroom braggarts, and even of certain Y.M.C.A. braggarts, to hint that some facts in the case were never given currency. The people who make this suggestion seldom indicate that they themselves are in possession of the truth; they imply that they know others who are. They say they have spoken to close friends of Gibbs, to policemen who talked off the record, to hospital attendants who examined the victim, to prisoners who knew Gibbs in the Lancaster County jail. They lift their eyebrows and then stare moodily into their beers or milkshakes. They give portentous nods. They lie. Certain information about Edward Gibbs and Marian Baker has been brought out here for the first time. Little of it will come as a surprise to the police or the prosecutor or the defense counsel. Some of these facts were not introduced at the trial because each attorney felt they might harm his own case. Brown and Ranck each had ready witnesses who were never used; the first, to testify to Gibbs' excellent character and previous blameless record; the second, to attest to his "sexy mood," as William Storb expressed it in court. But some of the facts were unknown to either lawyer. Unless there was some furtive witness lurking near the Harnish cottage that gray afternoon, someone who has failed to come forward and talk, we now know everything there is to be known about the crime. The rest of it lies buried in the decaying bodies of the murderer and his victim.

There is one remote possibility remaining. Gibbs might have confided in his parents, or in either Reverend Bollman or Reverend Guice. It is highly unlikely. The truth could not have disgraced him or his parents more; had he confided in them, they certainly would have communicated the new information to Brown, who might have used it accordingly. It is also hardly possible that either Bollman or Guice would have respected the custom of ministerial confidence above the outside chance of saving the young man's life. They too probably would have told Brown whatever they learned.

The versions of what caused Edward Gibbs to kill Marian Baker are almost as numerous as the people in Lancaster. Virtually each one is voiced with an air of authority; in the long-maintained inflexibility of the Pennsylvania Dutch character, each sounds impenetrably accurate when expounded by its champion. Voices quickly rise when the subject arises. Friendships have fallen apart because of it. Characteristically—in terms of Lancaster's personality, at least—those who know most, and who might be in the best position to speculate, will say the least. Until recently, Brown carefully avoided all reference to the case except in the company of his closest friends, who took pains to see that Gibbs was never brought into conversation when he was around. Ranck parried most questions with the response, "The case is closed." The Judge contained his customary judicial impartiality in absolute silence. There is one man in Lancaster, a tavernkeeper of great popularity, an ordinarily pleasantly loquacious fellow, who knows the Gibbs family well. He and his wife have visited them in Pitman, and the Gibbses have come to see them in Lancaster once or twice. When asked if he knows anything about the real story, he assumes a blank stare and shakes his head. Sometimes he has been heard to say, "There was more to it than a lot of people thought," but he has never insinuated that he knows it all. A stout, determinedly and unsuccessfully poker-faced fellow who loves the company of people, who reads widely and enjoys polemics, this man becomes distinctly uncomfortable when the Gibbs argument begins to flow up and down his bar; he goes off to one end by himself to watch the television, or he gruffly changes the course of the conversation. "I don't know why people want to go and make so much fuss about it," he once complained to a friend.

The fuss goes on and on, sustained in several versions. No one can say that one is more reliable than the next; no one, that is, except the proponents of each. They are as follows:

1. Edward Gibbs had been having an affair of long standing with Marian Baker. She had decided to break it off because she was engaged to Rankin and had not told him until that afternoon. He killed her in rage and grief.

2. Edward Gibbs was accused by Marian Baker of having got her with child. He killed her to eliminate the problem.

3. Edward Gibbs, having driven her to the Harnish

cottage, attempted to persuade Marian Baker to have intercourse with him. When she refused, he killed her for one of the following reasons:

(a) she had caused him to feel an irrepressible frustration;

(b) she had threatened to tell his wife;

(c) she had threatened to tell his fraternity brothers;

(d) she had threatened to blackmail him;

(e) he had, as he said so many times later, an impulse, pure and simple;

(f) she had threatened to send Edgar Rankin to deal with him;

(g) she had ridiculed him.

4. Edward Gibbs drove Marian Baker to the Harnish cottage and killed her in a fit of religious mania to punish her for her allegedly immoral behavior on the campus.

5. Edward Gibbs knew that Marian Baker had access to college funds. He suggested to her that she could contrive to slip him some in a petty embezzlement plan he had devised. When she refused and threatened to tell, he killed her.

6. Edward Gibbs killed Marian Baker because he thought she was carrying a large sum of money.

7. Marian Baker was performing what newspapers call an abnormal act upon Edward Gibbs. She bit him. Enraged, he killed her.

8. Edward Gibbs did not kill Marian Baker at all; he had read too many crime books, was deranged, and sought glory by the confession.

9. Marian Baker first tried to murder Edward Gibbs, and he killed her in self-defense.

10. Edward Gibbs was a disturbed, abnormal young man.

None of the foregoing can be proved except possibly

the last, to which three experts testified. It is the least popular of all the reconstructions, and the most scoffed-at. Insofar as the Lancaster mind and the procedure of the courts is concerned, Sigmund Freud and his followers might never have existed, and their work might well be considered as meaningless and unrelated to the ordinary course of life in this prosperous, ideally American community as the parlor tricks of Cagliostro. We are bound by the law, and we must believe in it and obey it. The law is of necessity empirical. It exists to protect those of us who are law-abiding against those who are not. If the law is to be carried out empirically, it is up to the officers of enforcement to interpret it empirically. Thus Ranck and Storb were behaving in an admirably efficient manner when they presented their case; they were behaving according to the experience of society as most of us know it and interpret its laws. The casework of the scientists of the mind to date has no validity, empirically speaking, in the courts. It has achieved some stature in isolated cases, but as psychiatrists are fond of saying, the law is, generally speaking, fifty years behind its time. The tendency to regard anyone "abnormal" as a "special" case, and not a familiar phenomenon, seems so firmly ingrained in our thoughts as to make it almost impossible for the law to be altered. And because the law cannot be altered, as yet, neither can our attitude toward such as Edward Gibbs. For this reason, and for the reason of the Jury's unwillingness to mitigate his sentence in the light of his abnormality as testified to by three experts, it must be concluded that his trial was a fair one. Certainly, as both Ranck and Brown have pointed out with excusable pride, it did not develop into a travesty or a carnival. It was conducted with dignified dispatch. So were the legal procedures that followed it.

Brown, hard hit by the verdict, set into motion the

legal machinery at once. On June twenty-sixth, he presented a motion for a new trial, arguing that the Court had erred in admitting the photographs of Marian Baker's body, the garter belt, and the pants; that the Court erred eight times in charging the Jury; and that the Court erred in permitting the District Attorney to recall Dr. Strecker for the purpose of asking him if Gibbs might kill again. Judge Wissler turned down this plea on August fourth. On August eighteenth, Gibbs was sentenced as follows:

> Now, August 18, 1950, the sentence of the law is that you, Edward Lester Gibbs, be taken hence by the Sheriff of Lancaster County to the jail of that county from whence you came, and from thence in due course to the Western Penitentiary in Centre County, Pennsylvania, and that you there suffer death during the week fixed by the Governor of the Commonwealth, in a building erected for the purpose on land owned by the Commonwealth, such punishment being inflicted by either the Warden or Deputy Warden of the Western Penitentiary, or by such person as the Warden shall designate, by causing to pass through your body a current of electricity sufficient to cause death and the application of such current to be continued until you are dead. May God in His infinite goodness have mercy on your soul.

Brown called in Thomas D. McBride, of Philadelphia, to assist in his efforts to save Gibbs. On October second, counsel asked the State Supreme Court for a new trial. The plea was denied on November twentieth. On December sixth, they asked the Supreme Court for a reargument of the case. It was refused on January 12,

1951. On January thirtieth, Governor John S. Fine set Gibbs' execution date in the week of April twenty-third. Now the defense attorneys turned to the Pardon Board, asking that the sentence be commuted to life imprisonment. The Board refused the plea on March twenty-first, and a second one on April eighteenth. Brown announced then that no further effort to save Gibbs would be made. Meanwhile, interested people made frantic efforts to get Governor Fine to commute Gibbs' sentence to life. If the Governor saw fit to examine the pleas, he made no public mention of it. His office repeatedly told the newspapers that no action would be taken in Gibbs' case. The arguments before the courts, the boards, and the Governor were all fairly similar. Brown and McBride continually re-emphasized Dr. Strecker's testimony as to Gibbs' irresponsibility and emotional immaturity. Ranck, in opposing them, reiterated his charge that sex was at the bottom of the case. The law being what it is, justice being what it is, and our attitude toward psychiatry being what it is, the learned gentlemen who reviewed the case saw no connection between the sexual attack, if any, and the underlying reasons for it. Gibbs was removed from the Lancaster County Prison to Rockview Penitentiary, Bellefonte, Pennsylvania, late in the afternoon of April twenty-first, a Saturday. He was taken there by four County officers, one of which was Deputy Sheriff Elmer Zerphey, who had escorted him back and forth from the Lancaster prison during his trial, and who had sat with him at counsel table. Zerphey and the boy seemed to have developed a liking for each other. As they said good-bye, Gibbs wished him a happy birthday; the deputy was to be fifty-three the next day. Zerphey said, "I'll never forget this birthday."

Early Sunday morning, Gibbs' head was shaved

and he was given, as a part of the State's inscrutable and single-minded devotion to routine, a physical examination. No one has yet learned why the latter was necessary, or if his execution might have been stayed if he had been suffering, say, a cold in the head, or even a heart condition.

On Sunday afternoon he was visited for the last time by his parents, who after their hour with him made arrangements to claim the body the following day. From then on he was with Reverend William Bollman almost continuously until the time of his execution. Dr. Bollman escorted him from the death row to the door of the chamber. He reported that Gibbs' last words were, "Give my love to my mother and father and tell them I'm all right." Dr. Bollman said, "He was remarkably composed, sustained by an unfaltering faith."

In the death chamber Gibbs was met by Reverend John W. Lenhardt, coincidentally a former resident of Lancaster city. Charles W. Fitzkee, *Intelligencer Journal* reporter, one of six newspapermen admitted among the twelve witnesses, wrote, "He entered the death chamber with head erect, flanked by two guards. He walked briskly to the chair, sat down and closed his eyes." Jerry Conn, of the *New Era,* wrote, "[he] went to his death with an almost weird lack of emotion. His face was an expressionless mask and his eyes were glazed. In fact, he gave a grim imitation of a mechanical man." Fitzkee later told a friend, "Ed Gibbs died like a man. He walked into that room with an expression on his face that seemed to say, 'Let's get this thing over with.' " Scarcely a minute and a half elapsed from the time Gibbs was led into the room until the executioner, Frank L. Wilson, of Pittsburgh, threw the switch that sent two thousand volts coursing three times through the body of the murderer. As Gibbs was being strapped into the chair and as the hood was put over his head, Chaplain Lenhardt intoned the Twenty-Third Psalm. Outside in the hall, Father Richard Walsh, the Catholic chaplain, was praying, and so were three men awaiting execution in the death row.

Throughout the Gibbs case the attitude of Lancaster people underwent several changes. When he first confessed, indignation prevailed. By the time he was brought to trial, the people had calmed somewhat. When the verdict was brought out by the Jury, there were many public expressions of satisfaction, some from people intimately connected with the case. Mrs. Leroy O'Donel, Marian Baker's aunt, quoted in the *Intelligencer Journal,* said, "Oh, that's the best thing that could have happened. We've been hoping and praying for it." Edgar Rankin said, "I think he got what he deserved. . . . He made a lot of people suffer and he should suffer himself." Rankin's father, however, said that he felt sorry for Gibbs' family. Donald Mylin, when interviewed, said, "I'm jubilant about the sentence. I slept last night for the first time in many weeks." Mylin emphasized that he was not speaking for the college; that morning, Dr. Theodore A. Distler had gone off to Florida, and he had made no comment before his departure. Mylin went on, "I have no malice in this case. I shudder at the thought that this boy's life must be taken. I'm the most chicken-hearted guy there is. But on the other hand, I think it's the best thing for the good of the whole public because this sentence is a far-reaching step to prevent these thrill and impulse killings that are menacing the whole American scene these days."

Both Lancaster dailies were flooded with letters beginning the day after the Jury reached its verdict. Some expressed approval, some sympathy. They were about equally divided. One cannot escape the feeling that most of them missed the point; that few of them showed any genuine understanding of the issues involved, or willingness to look beyond those presumedly Christian concepts by which so many of us live so rigidly. Even those that regretted the verdict seemed to have been written in blindness to the basic questions. Some letters indicated that the original indignation might have mounted between the time of Gibbs' arrest and his trial. One of these said:

Why so much sympathy for Gibbs? He was a real murderer. He confessed he was a low brow murderer . . . It's a disgrace on Lancaster County to let money walk away with pure downright murder. Is it right? No. Miss Baker's life was just as sweet and dear to her relatives, friends, and boyfriend that knew her as Gibbs' is. And how easy his death would be in the electric chair along side what Miss Baker went through. . . . So send him to the chair. It's the right place for him. If they don't . . . Lancaster has a right to open its prison doors and free everybody. What is the use in having laws if money is going to stand between how much more valuable Gibbs' life is than Miss Baker's.

A Daily Reader
Peach Bottom, Pa.

The Lancastrian instinct for economy seemed to rule many of the letter writers' feelings. A typical expression of this viewpoint said:

Congratulations are in order for the jury. . . . The Commonwealth and the people owe them a debt of gratitude for their courageous and just decree . . .

262

"It is not a simple or happy responsibility to condemn anyone to death, yet the electric chair is much more merciless and less horrible than the use of an automobile lug wrench. The maximum penalty allowed is far too mild . . . and fails entirely to serve as a deterrent to future crimes. . . .

"The people of the Commonwealth should realize . . . that this thoughtful jury has saved them thousands and thousands of dollars in taxes. The cost on maintaining the murderer in case of life sentence entails far more than the average man realizes. . . . He would be . . . much better off than millions . . . were in the last depression, and better off than many are at any time. . . .

"Nevertheless, Gibbs' defense attorney intends . . . to set aside the wisdom of the jury and the just demand of the Commonwealth. He proposes to sentence our people to support this murderer as long as he lives. He proposes leniency knowing that such action increases the likelihood of future recurrence of such and other crimes. . . .

"It is also high time that the courts know that our people are not deluded by the nonsense that 'My mind went blank.'

"It is quite a coincidence that the modern murderers' minds all 'go blank' and just as conveniently become rational again. That certainly is an overworked gag and defense counsel ought to think up something original . . ."

Henry Reitmann
Denver (Pa.)

263

In contrast was this sincere gush of Sunday School charity:

> As I sit here ready to write, I asked God to direct my hand with His judgment.
>
> I have a son . . . If my son should do a great wrong, I would expect to see him punished, but the death sentence would hurt me more than him. I would have to live all the rest of my life with a great weight in my heart. . . .
>
> I have daughters, too, and if one of them were harmed, I would expect to see justice done, but not the death sentence. At times, people did or said something wrong toward me, but I still like them. God's law is to forgive.

*

> I have seen how people suffered God's vengeance for wrong things they continually kept doing. It took a year or two in some cases, which was plenty of time to repent, but they repented not. One person died of a painful disease. The others had troubles in other ways. God took his vengeance with out man lifting a hand.

*

> After studying theology, could not Eddie Gibbs become a man like Paul?

*

> If our hearts burned with God's love . . . could we condemn a man not to live, to learn of such love, and to help others learn?
>
> Mrs. Richard Roland
> Willow Street, Pa.

The prevailing attitude in Lancaster was perhaps best summed up by an editorial in the *Intelligencer Journal* on March 17, 1950. It said, in part:

> The Gibbs trial has come to an end, and it seems altogether proper and fitting to commend everyone involved for the manner in which it was conducted.
> The case had all the elements needed to build it into a three-ring circus.
> But that didn't happen in Lancaster.
> And for that we are deeply grateful.

>   *

> The citizens of Lancaster County certainly should feel proud of their public officials in this instance.
> While by nature not revengeful, they must know that the law they live under and trust for protection demands an eye for an eye.
> A tragedy piled upon a tragedy is a horrible situation for most good citizens to contemplate, but that is the way of the law.

The indifference to psychiatric evidence on the part of the public is certainly not unusual. Antagonism to it, however, is something else; it is a bit more difficult to understand, considering the progress of education and the development of communication. Yet it exists, in Lancaster and in countless other communities. The antipsychiatry attitude was best expressed in a letter to the *New Era:*

> We are surely living in a strange world today. What has become of formerly universally accepted standards of right and wrong? Crime

no longer a sin, it would seem, but merely a momentary mental aberration, an emotional upheaval, a sort of brain-storm, a conveniently temporary form of insanity, accepted by muddle-headed juries as sufficient reason to bring in a verdict of "not guilty" . . . the time seems to have come when anyone can commit any crime on "impulse" with a more than fair chance of getting away with it.

When at the age of about six they began my course of religious instruction and training, my little catechism and my teachers told me the story of the Fall of Man and explained that, ever since that deplorable event, man's fallen nature has been fairly oozing evil impulses. But they also stressed the necessity of curbing, checking, subduing, overcoming these evil impulses. My dad—God rest his soul!—one of those sturdy Bavarians with old-fashioned ideas, must have taken his parental obligations seriously because, whenever his youngest offspring (yours truly) allowed any of his impulses to tempt him into mischief, the old gentleman would reach around the corner of the old family wardrobe for Das Spanische Roehrlein (. . . The stinging end of a buggy whip) and apply it with the grim determination to do his duty. Result: I soon learned to curb those "impulses" which, later in life, might have turned me into a killer or a sex-fiend.

If our learned friends, the psychiatrists . . . instead of looking for abnormal cerebrations, hidden motivations, obscure fixations, sporadic vacillations—or what else have you in the lexicon of psychiatry—were to go farther back, they would find that all this lack of impulse-control is owing directly to the lack of the old-fashioned application of Das Spanische Roehrlein. But, since it's too late for that when the case is already before judge and jury, the severe and just application of the law of compensation for sin and crime would surely help to curb similar "impulses" in other potential criminals.

Who can call his life safe in the future, if soft-headed juries continue to let crimes ascribed to so-called unaccountable impulses go unpunished?

Father William O.S.B.
St. Joseph's Hospital.

As though to go along with this point of view, the *New Era* ran an editorial that said partially:

There very likely is a place for psychiatry in a case like this, but we doubt that it is on the witness stand. Granted, as one of the experts remarked, it is not an exact science. In this instance it seemed scarcely a plausible guess.

Fortunately the jury refused to be confused. . . .

Society must thank that jury. Somewhere along the line society must call a halt to the growing contempt for law and common decencies that manifest (*sic*) itself in so many ways. The verdict in the Gibbs case will help immeasurably. We hope it sets a pattern. . . .

There can be no question but that the position of psychiatry almost invariably suffers because of the manner in which psychiatric evidence is presented in court. Operating under the law, Ranck had no choice but to attack and attempt to discredit the defense witnesses. Perhaps their case might have been aided if they had had more time with Gibbs, if their examinations had been more thorough. The blame for this must rest with them and with the defense attorney, but the blame is entirely hypothetical. Dr. Keyes, on the other hand, has been accused of minimizing Gibbs' condition simply to assist the Commonwealth's case. Sometime ago, asked what his position would have been had he been a witness for the defense, a role he had held on many occasions previously, he said that his testimony would have been the same. He had based his diagnosis, he said, on the definition of the passive-aggressive personality as outlined in Mental Disorders, a lexicon published by the American Psychiatric Association Mental Hospital Service. Both Drs. Keyes and Strecker had assisted in the compilation of this dictionary of disorder and disease. Dr. Keyes feels that justice was done in the Gibbs case, under the law as it now stands. He hastens to add that he is opposed to capital punishment. "Fundamentally, I am opposed to it," he has said, "but we must live under the law. I have never seen anyone deterred from murder because of fear of the electric chair or execution. I think we ought to do everything in our power to bring out the stupidity of capital punishment. We have no right to discuss the law, in a given case; all we can do is work and try to change it."

Dr. Strecker's point of view is opposed. He writes, "I do believe this trial represented a miscarriage of justice. In the first place there was very definite reason to believe outside my own conclusion, that Eddie Gibbs was a schizophrenic . . . Unfortunately, the opinion of the leading Rorschach expert in America (*Dr. Bruno Klopfer*

—*RG*) could not be introduced . . . because he could not appear in person. . . . Furthermore, there were other things which contributed to my opinion that the trial represented a miscarriage of justice. With all due respect to the District Attorney, he certainly 'waved the bloody rag.' He made a great deal of the horrible pictures of the murder and this, of course, does very much impress the jury. He belittled the Rorschach test in an undignified and scoffing manner, with no regard for the fact that this is a well-recognized and established test, used constantly in all first-class institutions of psychiatry. Finally, I do not believe a real motivation and premeditation was established. I think it was homicide based on psychopatholgy in which, in my opinion, while there might have been the capacity to distinguish intellectually between right and wrong, yet there was not the capacity to adhere to the right." Dr. Strecker is very probably wrong in the first part of his thesis. It is doubtful if the testimony of Dr. Klopfer would have done any more to sway the Jury in the face of the Commonwealth's conduct of the case.

It is generally felt in Lancaster that Dr. Strecker signed Gibbs' death warrant by answering Ranck's crucial question as to the possibility of Gibbs' killing again. Dr. Strecker gives these reasons for answering the question:

"I answered in the affirmative because in the first place it was an honest answer, based on the fact that pattern established by a lifelong psychopathology had not been changed and, therefore, for the protection of society, one would have to admit the possibility of the danger of homicide. I did not answer that I was a scientist, not a prophet, because after all an expert in any field, and particularly in a field of such close personal relationships as psychiatry, can only base his conclusions on skillful and thorough study. He has no way of predicting the margin of error which might exist, and therefore he cannot prophesy. I answered the question because I felt as a matter of conscience I was obliged to answer it. . . . My effort was to try to help to secure a just, intelligent, but at the same time, humane, and if I might say scientific verdict. I felt it would not be right for this man to be merely acquitted with the hazard that that might involve to society, and I also felt decidedly that execution would be morally and legally wrong."

Both Dr. Strecker and Dr. Keyes are in agreement on the ineffectuality of the current mode of presentation of psychiatric evidence in court. "I am very anxious," says Dr. Keyes, "that psychiatric testimony become a fair and useful instrument rather than a shuttlecock between attorneys in court." Dr. Strecker concurs. The two believe that it would be fairer to have a board of three qualified experts examine a man, and to hand down a report which could then be introduced as evidence of his mental condition.

A suggestion of this sort had been made to the District Attorney on January 25, 1950, by Dr. Elmer L. Horst, of Reading, Pennsylvania, a practicing psychiatrist and Chairman of the Mental Hygiene Committee of Berks County. Dr. Horst wrote:

"The psychiatrists of Pennsylvania are greatly disturbed about the employment of various psychiatrists in having their findings used to escape the law. Various members of the profession have suggested that psychiatrists appear only as friends of the court. I am sure that you, Mr. Brown, the Gibbs family and all concerned are desirous of seeing justice done in this instance. Both you and Mr. Brown would receive nation-wide recognition and the thanks of the medical and legal professions alike if you could agree to the following stipulations: either have court appoint a psychiatrist or several psychiatrists

270

to examine Mr. Gibbs and make their report directly to the court, or have the State and Defense each appoint a psychiatrist and have the court appoint a psychiatrist and have them combine their reports and present it to the court. . . . I do not wish to see psychiatrists become the laughing stock or the dumping grounds for problems which the legal profession cannot or will not face . . ."

This was one of the few sensible letters Ranck received in the course of his conduct of the case. He did not act on it because Brown had already engaged Dr. Strecker and he had already summoned Dr. Keyes. He did receive many other letters, however, and so did Brown. Some were congratulatory, some were downright condemnatory. Every crackpot in Lancaster felt called upon to express an opinion, generally unsigned, and every religious fanatic, and every person whose own emptiness could be temporarily filled by the writing of a letter. Some were not satisfied merely to write letters. Some felt called upon to seek out or to telephone members of the jury, the attorneys, the Gibbs family and their friends, and others who had remote connections with the case. The jury fared worst. One woman was called repeatedly late at night; when she would answer the telephone, a voice would say, "How do you feel, you murderer? Do you feel good, now that you've sent that poor boy to his death? May the Lord Jesus Christ have mercy on your soul." A Lancaster editor, months later, said with conviction, "The real victims in the Gibbs case were those people on the jury." The telephone calls went on for weeks afterward. It is popularly believed that they so affected one of the lady jurors that she had to be confined to bed. Strange stories and rumors about the jury arose; some of them are still heard in Lancaster bars, voiced with the same authority that characterizes those versions of what happened at the Harnish cottage. But not all the calls and visits were condemnatory. One lady juror says, "For weeks afterward, people came up to me, people I'd never seen before, and shook my hand. They said, 'I just want you to know how glad I am that you've made Lancaster safe for our daughters.' They said they thought we brought out a fair and honest verdict."

It is not exaggerating to say that virtually everyone in the area was affected by the trial. When this was suggested, some time later, to a well-read, intelligent man who is active in the social life of the community, he dismissed it as nonsense. Then he began to theorize. Within five minutes he was engaged in heated discussion, and the argument went on for an hour and a half. Sociologists and the psychiatrists might have some penetrating things to say about this kind of disinvolvement. It may be that their sciences are as yet too infantile to present us with any enduring conclusions.

Despite the commotion, the execution of Edward Gibbs seems to have accomplished nothing. It seems even to have taught very little. If it did teach anything, the lessons seem to have been badly learned both in Lancaster and in Pitman. It might be assumed that the case might have influenced both Pitman High and Franklin and Marshall College to assess themselves, and to take some precautions against the emergence of another supposedly normal, merely "spoiled" boy who will turn out to be an Edward Gibbs. Neither has done anything direct.

Principal Henry Cooper of Pitman High says, "The thing to do, of course, would be to have adequate, scientific means to identify potential Gibbses. That would take money, more money than we could dream of. But I would not say that the case was without impact on us. We do have sensitive members of the faculty; we try to hold the kids straight, try to help them find their way. And in my own bumbling way I use what small knowledge of psychology I have to help them."

Max Hannum, speaking for Franklin and Marshall, says, "There has been a tendency in colleges to go more and more heavily into guidance and testing programs, and we've followed that tendency, although possibly not because of the Gibbs case." No direct measures were adopted as a result of the case, Hannum added. The college still maintains the Guidance Center which once was operated jointly with the Veterans Administration. All freshmen are tested immediately they matriculate. All students on Probation for academic reasons are sent there for testing and assistance. The Center has a staff of seven, all of whom have teaching jobs. It may be that even a staff of seventy would not be enough to spot another Gibbs, for part of his sickness lay in his inherent inability to betray it. This is characteristic of this type of mental disorder.

Once the ordeal of his trial was past and the verdict had been handed down, Gibbs regained much of that studied, rigidly controlled respectability which he had been taught to present to the world at all times. To his guards at the Lancaster prison he seemed an intelligent, rational fellow. They sometimes played ball together, the guards and Gibbs and several others awaiting the pleasure of society. John Ranck remembers his last sight of Gibbs in the flesh with a mixture of awe and puzzlement. He had gone out to the jail and while waiting to transact his business chanced to look out a window into the recreation area. There were Gibbs and two prisoners and a guard enjoying a game of rounders. The guard was catching, one prisoner was batting, another was fielding, and Gibbs was pitching. Gibbs' stance was professional. He faced the batter like a big-leaguer, now and again casting a cautious look over his shoulder at first base. He was, in every physical aspect, the normal American boy dreaming of the days when a scout would see him on the lot and send him up for a tryout. Ranck wondered, at the time, how he could have done what he did. Gibbs wore his cloak of normality at all times. He never seemed morose; his disposition, everyone at the prison said, was cheerful. He was making the best of it. At Christmas time, with his fate still undecided, he sent out cards to his friends.

8

Post Script

If you are members of a prominent Pitman, New Jersey, family, people of standing and substance in the community, active in its commerce and church and charities, and you have lost a son, what do you do? Why, you follow to the letter the rules for proper behavior—the rules of Pitman, New Jersey, of Lancaster, Pennsylvania, or of any other village or city in this rules-conscious, rules-abiding country. There is nothing else to do and maintain your position. J. Lester and Florence Gibbs made arrangements for their Eddie's funeral shortly after they returned from their last sight of him. They sent out, an acquaintance estimates, some one hundred and fifty invitations, using the standard issue of the S. E. Burkett Funeral Home, 30 West Holly Avenue, Pitman. At the top of each invitation, under a silver-grey border of four horizontal lines, was the legend, *"In Profound Sorrow We Announce the Death of,"* and beneath that was handwritten "Edward Lester Gibbs." The date of death, also handwritten, followed; then came S. E. Burkett's address, printed. Beside it was the handwritten word "Private," underlined. Below

275

was the date of the funeral, Thursday, April 26, 1951; the time, one-thirty P.M. and the place of interment, Hillcrest, a cemetery located just northeast of Pitman on Delsea Drive, Route 47. The ceremonies could not have been conducted with more sedulous attention to niceties. The parents' behavior, everyone said, was flawless. Each bore up admirably, J. Lester in a subdued suit, Florence in a simple print dress. The Reverend William Bollman, D.D., of Lancaster, and the Reverend Marvin Guice, of Pitman, officiated at the services, the brevity of which in no way mitigated their essential dignity. Dr. Bollman spoke briefly on Gibbs' honorable, spiritual character as it had been revealed during their meditations. Mr. Guice delivered the customary benediction. The mourners were composed; they wept quietly when overcome, but allowed no demonstrations to disturb the serenity of the two rooms Burkett's had made available. To some, the scene was particularly affecting because the casket was open. Edward Gibbs lay as though at peace, unaware that he was at last getting some of the attention he had always craved so desperately. The lips were closed over the protruding teeth. The face seemed to have lost some of the fullness which had been noticeable in the pictures taken of him while he was awaiting his doom. The charred and shaven skull was concealed by a white cloth cap similar to one that a surgeon wears. The pallbearers were all old friends; there was one fraternity brother. Someone said that Eddie had chosen them himself in his final meeting with his parents.

After the coffin was lowered into the hole at Hillcrest, some of the celebrants went back to the Gibbs house at 48 North Oak Avenue, where a buffet awaited them. There was a ham, the usual variety of relishes, and a potato salad so superior it moved several of the ladies to compliment their hostess. She seemed abstractedly pleased. The guests made small talk. A few remarked, when they were safely out of hearing, that Les and Florence really were taking this whole thing very well. It was surprising, someone said. Mrs. Gibbs' graciousness may be remembered by some as long as they remember their first staggering sight of the open casket. One member of the party can still remember a warm little speech of welcome she made at the undertaker's an hour or so before the services commenced. "Oh, R——," said Mrs. Gibbs to this person, "how *nice* of you to come. I'm so glad. Now," she added, leading the way with a quick little step, "come and see our Eddie. He's finally back home."

The end.

Note

While assembling the material from which this book is made I was frequently asked why I felt bound to reconstruct the Gibbs case. I could not answer specifically; I hope the answer lies in the pages preceding. I should like to thank the many people who assisted me, but I must refrain from mentioning their names. There are others whose physical assistance and moral backing must be acknowledged, however, among them Charlotte Jeffries Reinhold, who extracted the bones of the case from the newspaper files; Tony Marshall, whose continuing aid in the early stages was invaluable; Theodore S. Amussen, who grasped the nature of the project from the beginning; and Robert Loomis and Maxwell Wilkinson, who were unrelenting in their encouragement. I should also like to thank Earl E. Keyser, editor of the *Intelligencer Journal*, and Lancaster Newspapers, Inc., for permission to use the copious quotations. To Mary E. Marshall I offer my gratitude for her comments on the rough manuscript and her hospitality during the time in which the bulk of the book was written.

Lancaster, Pennsylvania: November 1953

R.G.

278